on track ...

The Jam

every album, every song

Stan Jeffries

sonicbondpublishing.com

Sonicbond Publishing Limited
www.sonicbondpublishing.co.uk
Email: info@sonicbondpublishing.co.uk

First Published in the United Kingdom 2023
First Published in the United States 2023

British Library Cataloguing in Publication Data:
A Catalogue record for this book is available from the British Library

Copyright Stan Jeffries 2023

ISBN 978-1-78952-299-0

Typeset in ITC Garamond Std & ITC Avant Garde Gothic
Printed and bound in England

Graphic design and typesetting: Full Moon Media

Follow us on social media:
Twitter: https://twitter.com/SonicbondP
Instagram: www.instagram.com/sonicbondpublishing_/
Facebook: www.facebook.com/SonicbondPublishing/

Linktree QR code:

on track ...
The Jam

every album, every song

Stan Jeffries

sonicbondpublishing.com

Acknowledgements

To begin with, I would like to thank Richard Hunter. In the spring of 2022, he gave me a slim volume detailing all you'd really need to know about the *Carry On* films. It was my hugely enjoyable summer read. At the end of the book were listed other titles from the publisher, Sonicbond, and an open invitation to readers that if they had an idea and could write well enough to make their idea a readable reality, then to get in touch.

Which leads me to the author of that *Carry On* book and Sonicbond owner, Stephen Lambe. I emailed Stephen and said I reckoned I could have a decent crack at a book about The Jam. He replied and said I should go for it. I'm very grateful for the trust and faith he put in me with that email, and I hope I have done justice to both him and the *On Track* series.

To Sumiko Oshima, I want to say thanks for looking over an early manuscript for its 'readability'. Her eye for detail and for pushing me towards clarity has been most welcome.

To Adam Hiles, one-time guitarist in Newcastle combo yourcodenameis: milo and latterly Tank Engine, for his technical insight and correcting my musical mistakes without laughing at me.

To Steven Arbon-Davis for his remembrances, input and research on my behalf when he should have been enjoying his holiday.

A huge thank you to Mick Marston for his wise counsel. When I began this book, I'd forgotten how much is required of a writer (my previous stab at writing was over two decades ago, and the mind draws a veil over such stressful memories). Without Mick's patience, the incredible generosity of his time, his different ways of looking at the songs and his general willingness to read everything I wrote, and then to offer creative and constructive opinion has been invaluable. More than once, he steered me out of cul-de-sacs and onto the open road. He questioned why I'd written something, and questioned whether I should have written it at all. The effort he gave to the project was beyond anything I could have hoped for, and for that, I am eternally grateful.

And finally, for her belief, sarcasm, derisory laughter, technical knowledge of the video medium, and skill with the English language, I would like to thank Helen. Obvs.

Stan Jeffries
Arroyo De La Miel (Málaga)
September 2023

'All Around The World', arranged by Ziggy Ludvigsen. Included are the author's handy 'this is an A, and this is a G' chord diagrams. It was my early days as a guitarist.

on track ...
The Jam

Contents

SIDE A	RECORDING DATES MONTH.YEAR
1. NON-STOP DANCING	(05.76)
2. LEFT, RIGHT AND CENTRE	(05.76)
3. AGAIN	(10.75)
4. ONE HUNDRED WAYS	(03.76)
5. FOREVER AND ALWAYS	(03.75)
6. I WILL BE THERE	(03.75)
SIDE B	
1. WHEN I NEEDED YOU	(12.75)
2. PLEASE DON'T TREAT ME BAD	(12.75)
3. SOUL DANCE	(05.76)
4. I GOT BY IN TIME	(05.76)
5. WONDERFUL WORLD	(04.80)
6. ISOLATION	(04.80)

The track listing of *When We Were Young*. Early versions of 'Non-Stop Dancing' and 'I Got By In Time' are painfully slow. Both feature rolling R&B piano and an alarming American accented vocal from Weller.

We Were Young And Full Of Ideas – An Introduction

I must start with a confession. I only 'found' The Jam at the time of *All Mod Cons*. Before you write me off as a Johnny come lately, let me explain.

By the time The Jam had settled as the three-piece we all know and were playing the pubs and toilets of 1976 London, I was an 11-year-old living in my hometown of Sheffield. Punk had made itself known in the city (pardon the pun) and a few local bands tried their hand, but the venues remained a long way out of reach to me. There was music in my house; Elvis, my mum's Andy Williams, Jack Jones, Vicki Carr and other easy listeners, and my dad's scratchy Dixieland Jazz 78s. My brother, three years older, dabbled with glam and owned records by The Sweet, Slade and The Glitter Band, and we had, like many families, 'Bohemian Rhapsody', a song I loathed at the time but have since grown to appreciate, if not exactly like. But, for me, it was clear that this was not what I was after.

For years past, I had joined the millions who every week tuned in to watch Britain's most popular music show, *Top Of The Pops*. As The Jam made their debut in May 1977 with their first single, 'In The City', I must have seen them, but it clearly failed to register. I also remember ex-mod and glam royalty Marc Bolan introducing them on his TV show *Marc* in the summer of the same year. And whilst I remember Bolan's introduction mainly because he called the band 'Jam', I don't remember the band's performance of 'All Around The World', their second single. A quick scan of everyone's favourite memory jogger, the internet, reveals Bolan's full introduction:

Alright. Welcome to a new show called *Marc*. There'll be a lot of new sounds, a lot of new experiences. The biggest and best so far this week is an amazing group called ... Jam.

Fast forward a year or two and by early 1979, I knew about *All Mod Cons*. In April, on my 14th birthday, my parents gave me a Rickenbacker 4001 bass copy because Bruce Foxton played a Rickenbacker 4001. (I was delighted when I later found pictures of John Entwistle and Paul McCartney playing the same model.) It was another month before I got an amp – 'We're not made of money, son' – but if you hit the strings hard enough, you could hear the notes. I confined myself to my bedroom and, within a fortnight or so, had learned the bass lines to the album. And that was my foray as a musician for the time being, though it was to reappear some years later.

For now, I threw myself into all things mod, and Weller was my guru. I knew of The Beatles, of course, but now I had the Small Faces, The Yardbirds, Spencer Davis Group, The Kinks, The Creation and The Action; Stax and Motown; Jamaican ska ('63-'67 only, after that it wasn't ska anymore) and northern soul. I somehow convinced my dad that I had to have a black and white dogtooth check suit and it had to be bought from Carnaby Cavern on Carnaby Street in London because I'd seen the adverts in the nation's top music paper *New Musical Express* (*NME*) which gave legitimacy to my purchase. And so, train tickets were bought, and the suit was acquired. I found a US fishtail parka in a Sheffield Army & Navy store and bought Fred Perry polos and button-down shirts (to this day, I only buy button-down shirts, old habits and all that). I was never sure, when I used to insist on wearing a tie to go to the local shops, if my mum was proud of me or thought I was nuts. In 1982, I reached the obvious pinnacle of mod culture, using the wages from my first job to buy a Lambretta Li150. (Statement: The Lambretta is waaay cooler than the Vespa. Discuss.) That job happened to be as a technician apprentice at the Ministry of Defence, popularly shortened to MOD. It was a continual source of amusement to my friends.

Following *All Mod Cons,* The Jam released *Setting Sons*, arguably my favourite album, though I argue with myself about this a fair bit, *Sound Affects* and *The Gift*. Whilst The Jam were a going concern, I saw them play six times. Not many times, some of you may reasonably argue, but considering my age at the time, I would contend that it was not bad. The last show I saw was on Tuesday, 7 October 1982, at Manchester Apollo, the fourth last gig the band ever played. National Express laid on a coach for the gig and I went with my mate, Barney. It was raining hard, unsurprising given the time of year and the city, and, in the hundred or so yards between coach and venue, we got soaked to the skin. On the previous occasions of watching The Jam play, I'd been down the front, in the middle of the frightening crush of bodies, but this time Barney and I stood at the back and watched, properly watched, for the first time.

And then it was over, I was still only 17 and Paul Weller, incredibly, when you look back at the songs he wrote, was still only 24. I continued my devotion to Weller by becoming an ardent fan of The Style Council, joining the fan club and buying everything released on his own Respond record label, but, eventually and inevitably, my contemporary musical love moved on to others. By now, I had sold the Lambretta, learnt the guitar and, in time, bought an Epiphone Casino as played by John Lennon in the *Get Back* films and, in the Style Council and as a solo artist, Weller himself. With my first band, our set included 'It's Too Bad' from the *All Mod Cons* album and later, when I began my career in the music industry, working for bands as a tour manager and backline technician (or 'tech' for brevity and please, don't call them 'roadies', it's not 1972) I would line check the bass with 'It's Too Bad' (old habits and all that.) As I travelled the world, the job enabled me to buy Jam records and CDs in such unlikely places as Los Angeles, Sydney and Tokyo.

I tell you all this not because I think you may be interested in a potted version of my life story, but to show how much The Jam meant to me at the time, and how you can draw a line back through both my taste in music and my choice of career to the band. John Lennon, in 1966, famously said, 'Before Elvis, there was nothing'. For me, before The Jam, there was nothing.

If We Communicate For Two Minutes Only – About This Book

Let me first say that I've never met the band. Unless you take into account one memorable Sunday afternoon in 1980 when, as a gaggle of us who'd been waiting outside Sheffield Top Rank from the earlyish hours, we were let into the band's soundcheck later that afternoon. I would, and do, certainly call it a 'meeting', but in reality, it was simply a chance to get a few autographs (for me, it was the cover to 'When You're Young') and ask what we considered desperately important questions but were, in retrospect, as banal as might be expected from a group that seemed to be mainly comprised of 14-year-olds. A favourite was 'When's the album out?' (referring to *Sound Affects*), which was asked so many times that in the end, Weller sighed, 'I should have the date written on my fucking forehead'.

At the time, I thought I'd been incredibly lucky to be allowed into that soundcheck. What I didn't realise was it was standard practice for the band, as Weller explained in the documentary *The Making Of All Mod Cons*:

> We're not talking about two or three people; we're talking about hundreds of people, sometimes three or four hundred. It was almost like doing a matinee in the afternoon. That was us trying to build bridges between us and the audience and breaking down this rock star mystique bollocks. I think that counted for an awful lot for those people who were there. Those things stay with you as you grow up.

And he's right. That afternoon meant a great deal to me and still does.

As that was, and is still, my only direct contact with any member of The Jam, I haven't had the chance to ask their opinions of the songs, so other than what has already been recorded in interviews, I give you my own opinions. As this book isn't intended as some kind of hagiography, it isn't all sweetness and light, there is criticism, but I hope it's valid. I believe it is.

Some readers may find my focus on the band's artwork and videos a little longwinded, but I believe that everything together makes a band what they are and as we will see, Weller had some input in this regard, sometimes costing the band thousands of pounds because of changes he wanted to make to album sleeves. And besides, as we live in an age where the question is likely to be, 'Have you seen the new video?' rather than 'Have you heard the new song?' the image of an artist is more important than ever. None more so than for The Jam in 1977, when their mod aesthetic certainly made them stand apart from the punk crowd.

From time to time, I've used contemporary quotes from the band or from journalists, to illustrate the prevailing thoughts of the day but those aside, these are my remembrances and, after 40 years of listening to these songs, what I take from them now. I've also used copious lyrics because there were few artists around at the time who cared as much about their lyrics as Weller, and talking about Jam songs without referring to the lyrics wouldn't make any sense. Again, although much has already been written about Weller's words, at times, I've interpreted them in my own way.

As music is, like all the arts, subjective, I don't expect everyone to agree with everything I say, many of you will have your own memories and younger readers their own ideas, but that's where we are and if anyone wants to spend an afternoon in the pub telling me I've got the wrong end of the stick about 'Thick As Thieves', then I'm all ears.

The songs in this book all appeared on official releases, and either made the charts in their own right or were part of a package at the time. This means that tracks appearing on imports, EPs or extras are included. There are also remarks about post-career Jam albums and compilations *Dig The New Breed, Snap!, Direction, Reaction, Creation, Extras* and the covers album *Fire & Skill*. Since, for the most part on these albums, they are simply the same tracks as on the singles and albums and have therefore already been written about, those tracks have been passed over, but there are some interesting demos and cover versions that never saw the light of day during The Jam years, and I've made comments about those. There are other Jam compilations available of the *Greatest Hits* variety, but I've chosen to ignore them as they add nothing different in terms of songs or production. I have tried to include in each individual entry when a track has appeared in films or TV shows and dramas to show the overreaching influence of the band through the years. If a reader is aware of an omission that they consider an egregious oversight in this respect, I can only apologise.

I've approached the songs in chronological order, but singles that are part of an album are dealt with within the text of the album so, although 'In The City' was the band's first release, I talk about it as part of the *In The City* album which makes it the seventh song to be discussed. My reasoning behind this is I think that the order of songs on an album, particularly in the pre-digital age where the listener couldn't easily jump around and skip tracks to their heart's content, would be something a band or artist would think long and hard about, and take some time deciding on the track listing; which song opened and closed the album and, as importantly in my view, which song closed side A and which began side B. B-sides of singles will be dealt with after the album on which the A-side appears.

Some song titles will be abbreviated in the form that, to my way of thinking, all Jam fans abbreviate them. Therefore, after the first mention, 'The Bitterest Pill (I Ever Had To Swallow)', becomes 'Bitterest Pill', much, I'm sure, to everyone's relief, and 'Tube Station' becomes just that. All of The Jam's output was on Polydor Records (except where stated) and release dates, where they differ in various books and magazines, are taken from official Polydor publications. Also, in the technical information of the singles and albums, I've included a catalogue number (cat. no.).

I've tried to stay away from muso-wankeryness as far as possible, but after playing in and working for bands for the last 40 years, I'm afraid a little of this will inevitably seep in. Gigs, for me, can be something of a busman's holiday and I bring that with me when I listen to music. I will, however, keep that sort of thing short and use it only when I think it will add to the narrative. A bit like a Weller guitar solo.

Band Credits

Finally, the personnel on these songs are Paul Weller (guitar), Bruce Foxton (bass) and Rick Buckler (drums). From time to time, each band member would add a little something different (harmonica, piano, accordion) and, where known, these are credited in the text. Occasionally, especially towards the end of the band's career, guest musicians appeared, and these will be accredited as they were on the releases. I apologise to anyone who appeared on these records who has been omitted.

Absolute Beginners – 1972-1977

In 1972, popular music in Britain could broadly be divided into an unholy triumvirate: glam rock, prog rock and heavy metal. Glam rock consisted mainly of groups of men past their youthful prime who had given it a go in the sixties as Beatles wannabees or pure R&B acolytes who'd taken the 12-bar blues formula, ramped it up, grown their hair, grown flares and grown rich parodying themselves. That some of these acts turned out to have some musical integrity (Slade and Sweet being the most obvious) appears rather by accident than design.

Progressive rock (prog rock) was, to my admittedly less than extensive knowledge, exclusively men, but these men had university degrees and knew more than basic rock and roll riffs, and that wasn't a good thing. Whereas glam rock might bring a smile to your face as you stomped around in dangerously elevated boots, prog rock wasn't intended to make you smile, dance, or do anything other than (lazy stereotype alert!) lounge around your shared student house, contemplating life on other planets and how any one song could ever be spun out to more than 20 minutes long. The answer to the last question was to use an astonishing number of complicated chord structures and sequences which had the consequence, or perhaps the intention, of making the music impossibly difficult to play.

The heavy metal brigade was more simplistic than even the glam rockers; double denim, supercharged blues riffs, long hair and a visceral delivery from a front man in jeans so tight you could count the veins, they took the 12-bar method and gave it some real welly. That some of these groups became worldwide and long-lasting music legends is a testament to the fact that a simple tune played with a degree of passion will always hit the right nerve.

Back in 1972, on a Thursday evening in Woking, a suburb 20 miles to the south of London, cold because winter was setting in, the patrons of a working men's club were about to witness the first gig by two young kids, barely into their teens. They had a set of six songs, all covers, the last of which was a Chuck Berry number. The audience took little notice but applauded politely as they knew the father of one of the boys. Paul Weller and his best friend Steve Brookes had played their first gig. The father was John Weller, Paul's dad, and he became The Jam's manager for the duration of their career.

Weller was 14 years old when he took that first step, became hooked on the buzz that you get when you're on stage, and never let the feeling go. Within a year, the duo had met other like-minded musicians, all from the same school in Woking, Sheerwater County Secondary, and Weller and Brookes had begun writing their own songs, most of them Beatles pastiches because, at the time, Weller listened to little else. Within a year, the band had become a four-piece, Weller playing bass as one of those like-minded musicians, Dave Waller, had arrived with his guitar and another Sheerwater pupil, Neil Harris, played drums. By now, the band had a name, though the etymology is disputed: either it was simply because of the jam sessions the band had at school, or it was Nicky Weller, Paul's sister, who suggested it one morning over the breakfast table. Whatever the reality, The Jam it was.

In the summer of 1973, Harris left the band and was replaced by Rick Buckler and by the end of the year, Waller had left to try to carve out a career writing poetry. The following year, the band advertised for another guitarist, and, on the recommendation of Harris, Bruce Foxton joined. By the end of 1974, Weller and Foxton had swapped instruments. It was also in 1974 that Weller first heard The Who song 'My Generation' and learned about mods, and for him personally, things started to fall into place. Mod, Weller said, 'would give me a base and an angle to write from'. But it was more than just a passing interest. Matching black suits and Weller's first Rickenbacker 330 (bought primarily because Pete Townshend played the same, it was the guitar of choice for many 1960s mod groups) gave The Jam a 'look'. Though it was a look that was to make them instantly different to the punks who appeared a year or two later, it also became a stick to beat them with by many critics.

By early 1975, the band had become proficient enough to audition for EMI, though the label passed on the chance to sign what would become the biggest band in the UK. More importantly, Weller had discovered Dr. Feelgood and began to style his playing on the choppy rhythm/lead of the band's guitarist, Wilko Johnson. Indeed, you can clearly see on some early TV performances Weller steals something from Johnson's on-stage actions. With the departure of Waller, and after unsuccessful auditions for a second guitarist, the band remained a three-piece, though still not feeling entirely settled with the format.

In 1976, Weller saw the Sex Pistols play and his writing, and the band's playing, attained a focus; mod styles played with punk ferocity. Seeing The Clash showed Weller that lyrics could say something about politics, and that idea became The Jam's calling card; at his height, no one wrote songs that were so socially and politically acutely observed than Paul Weller.

Looking to add to the band's line-up, an advert was placed for a keyboard player, but there were no successful applicants and, finally, the band settled as a three-piece. Still without a record deal, they played as many shows as John Weller could arrange whilst Foxton, always more cautious than his bandmates, held on to his job as a printer. In October 1976, the band played a gig on the streets of Soho Market and by then had gained enough interest from the media that the show was reviewed in music papers *Melody Maker* and *Sounds*, ('could do with a bit more originality' opined the latter) as well as the fanzine *Sniffin' Glue*, a magazine with which Weller would have a spectacular falling out within months after it wrote The Jam spent too much time on stage tuning their instruments and described them as being 'tighter than the London Symphony Orchestra'. Quite the crime. Being discordant is one thing; personally, that's a sound I like, but being out of tune is something entirely different and no one can listen to a band play out of tune and not find it rubbish. Those were the times of punk, though, and hipsters will have their opinions. The quote led to Weller burning a copy of the fanzine on stage.

In January 1977, after the *NME* had reviewed a live show at London's 100 Club as 'exceedingly promising', Polydor A&R man Chris Parry saw them at another London venue, the Marquee. With half a mind on the fact that Polydor had already missed out on the Pistols and the Clash, he quickly signed the band – for the princely sum of £6,000 – and it was duly reported in the press, 'Polydor climb aboard the new-wave bandwagon'. For the 18-year-old Weller, though, it was the culmination of his dreams. The only thing left now was to be bigger than The Beatles.

```
Hate is now respectable,
Hate is neon and chrome,
Shiny and exciting.
Accelerating into your home,
Via - wine.


Murder on the terraces,
Foots in high places,
And its all true,
its all here in black and white,
its all so sickening,
and we're so satisfied.


A torture bulletin every half-hour,
Death in Turkey, Spain, London, New York City,
Death is your T.V.
Hate is death,
and death is good for selling soap powder.
```

A Dave Waller poem from the *In The City* songbook. The second verse was rearranged by Weller for 'In The Street Today' from the *This Is The Modern World* album. I assume 'Foots in high places' is a typo.

'1-2-3-4!' In The City To All Around The World

In The City (1977)

LP: cat. no. 2383 447
Recorded at Stratford Place Studios
Produced by Chris Parry and Vic Smith
UK release date: 20 May 1977
Highest UK chart placing: 20

By the time The Jam had signed to Polydor at the beginning of 1977, the band line-up had been Weller, Foxton and Buckler for almost two years and had played hundreds of shows, honing their songs into two- and three-minute blasts of pure energy, and they knew their set so well it was a case of going into the studio and recreating the live sound as far as possible. Recorded in only 11 days, with Parry taking the lead role because, as Foxton remembered, 'We were all just in awe of it (the recording process)', the album is basically the pick of the band's live set and, in that respect, does its job admirably, though Weller later stated that he was unhappy with the finished article. This critical approach to their own work became a repeating factor throughout the band's recording career.

The album is taut, tight, brash and breathless. It's the sound of a band who know what they're doing musically and are going about achieving it in a very straightforward manner, though that did result in a fairly one-dimensional record, which makes it a lot easier to listen to than to write about. Despite, or more likely because of, the basic nature of the recording, the album received good reviews, and though one or two reflected on Weller's youth obsession, 'their teen-orientated 'rebel' lyric pose', they all noted just how good The Jam were musically; they could actually play. Phil McNeill in the *NME* mentioned the obvious influences of Pete Townshend and Wilko Johnson but sees through the bluster and comes to the point, 'The Jam's commercial potential is enormous'. There is, however, a prescient warning from Chas de Whalley in *Sounds*:

The Jam certainly have it in them to do great things but somebody's trying to get too much out of it much too soon.

That became clear with the release of the band's second album, but we're getting ahead of ourselves.

In The City reached number 20 in the charts, selling 60,000 copies in the first week, a more than respectable position for a relatively unknown band. It's interesting to note that the group might have identified with punk, citing the Sex Pistols and The Clash as influences, but none of the early reviews of The Jam call them punk, but rather new wave. In retrospect, the point is moot because, by the time the band recorded their third album, the only thing they really sounded like was themselves, and other bands began to copy the 'Jam sound'.

In The City ticks all the boxes that Weller and The Jam employed for the remainder of the band's career: Weller and Foxton exchanging lines in classic R&B 'call and response' and duetting a la Lennon and McCartney; 'oohs' and 'aahs' (initially sounding distinctly out of place given the times they were playing in and the audiences they were playing to); swearing, which Weller does often and with gusto, even managing to sneak milder swear words into Top Ten singles and, at the very end, a number one single; Weller scratching his plectrum along the bottom E string (the fat string) and switching between pick-ups to give the 'Morse code' sound that Pete Townshend used so effectively on The Who's 'Anyway, Anywhere, Anyhow' single; and the juxtaposition of city and country, urban and rural.

For the album sleeve, Polydor art director Bill Smith wanted an urban landscape so chose white tiles with a graffiti logo. The photographer, Martyn Goddard (who went on to work with the band many times) remembered how difficult that would have been:

I thought of all the problems a location shoot would incur because of the need to spray paint on a wall and the permissions and permits that would be required.

After agreeing that the shoot should take place in his own studio, Goddard and Smith stuck tiles over two 8'x4' flats (pieces of wood or board used for backdrops in theatres). Goddard:

I can't remember whether it was budget or time constraints, but Bill and I tiled the flats the morning of the session, and it was Bill who took the black spray paint and, in one attempt, produced the iconic logo on the white ceramic tiles as the glue was setting.

It was a logo that appeared as actual graffiti across the walls of the nation, though if you were a law-abiding 14-year-old, you made do with your schoolbooks. The logo takes the top half of the sleeve, the bottom being a suitably moody band shot. As if to prove his punk credentials, Weller wore a button badge of The Damned, the band credited with releasing the first punk single, 'New Rose', on 22 October 1976. The back of the sleeve shows Weller mid-leap and mid-Townshend windmill, Buckler shielding his eyes from the sun (despite being indoors and wearing sunglasses), and Foxton displaying alarmingly flared suit trousers. To add to the inner-city feel, there are a few smashed tiles, presumably to reflect urban decay. It's average stuff and the group became more involved in the band's artwork as the years passed.

What I was unsure about, due to my buying the album over 18 months after release, was whether my plain white inner sleeve was standard as each subsequent album had the lyrics printed. A straw poll of my contemporaries suggests it was, though the US release had an insert with random lines taken from songs and typed onto 'tickertape'. Certain words were highlighted in these lines, including a helpful circling of 'shit'. Which is a professional design department's equivalence of underlining the naughty words in a dictionary.

To promote the album the band were booked onto The Clash's *White Riot* tour beginning in May 1977 but only three dates in, chaos ensued. The audiences were doing the same as the Teddy Boys two decades previously and ripping out the seats of the venues, there were arguments between The Jam and The Clash over soundchecks, and The Jam's £100 a night fee was withheld as the £1,000 tour buy on from Polydor never appeared. (Having worked in the live side of the music business, I've always found the idea of buying a place on a tour to be questionable. The headline either wants a band to support them or they don't. And paying to be on a tour is one of the shoddier aspects of a generally shoddy industry.) As a result of the band leaving the tour, new dates were quickly organised for June and July and The Jam set out on their first nationwide headline tour. 42 dates were booked, but only 36 were completed as playing that number of shows with the energy the band gave to their live set night after night was never a realistic probability, and during the run, dates were cancelled to allow them to recover.

'Art School' (Weller)

A four-chord intro and a suitably aggressive punk '1, 2, 3, 4!' introduce the album and off it speeds, and barely lets up for the next 30 minutes or so. 'Art School' is a working-class paean that tells us the old bunch of middle-class art schoolers have had their day and it's 'us' who are going to take over. It's a nice thought, and full of the youthful fire you'd expect from a 17-year-old raging against prog-rock hippies. Musically, it's the simplest song on the album (including 'Batman'), though the lyrics are sometimes a tad confusing as Weller sings, apparently without irony, 'wear any clothes just so long as they're bright', this from a band making a name for themselves with monochrome stage wear.

Surprisingly, especially for 1977, the track has its own video (or 'promo film' in the language of the time), which would imply the song was earmarked as a single, but I've never read anything that would suggest this was the case. The promo follows a pattern that became familiar for Jam videos, until perhaps 'Going Underground', in which very little thought appears to be put into the filming; it's the three of them playing the song. Here though, there is something more to catch the eye as in the background are three, what we presume to be art students, painting various words ('Now' with the 'o' having an arrow in classic Who logo style) and attacking the three giant canvasses with Jackson Pollock-esque slashes and flicks of paint. Perhaps this was a homage to 1960s proto-psychedelists The Creation, who used to paint canvases on stage while performing the song 'Painter Man' – covered a decade later by Teutonic disco titans Boney M. Was it a homage? Maybe it was just The Jam being overly literal; art = paint, which is something that the band could be accused of time and again as the years and the videos passed. [Check out The Creation's 1967 appearance on German pop show *Beat Club,* where singer Kenny Pickett takes the opportunity of the guitar solo to slash paint across a perspex screen positioned so it seems he's painting the TV camera – so psychedelic. The solo itself sees guitarist Eddie Phillips using a violin bow, years before Jimmy Page took the idea.]

Visually The Jam's video tells us everything about the band's style; Rickenbackers to the fore, dressed in matching white trousers and 'Jam shoes', and Weller sporting a black jumper with an impossible-to-make-out design in black electrician's tape. This was a trick Roger Daltrey used at the start of The Who's career when playing live, using pop art tropes that were de-rigueur at the time, and Weller uses the same style on the cover of The Jam's second album, *This Is The Modern World.* The performance itself is a suitable introduction to The Jam live; intensity, aggression, passion and lyrics that spoke openly to the fans who were very quickly getting into the band in larger and larger numbers,

Do what you want if it takes your mind,
Better do it now, 'cos you won't have time,
And never worry if people laugh at you,
The fools only laugh 'cos they envy you.

As the song drops into a middle-eight, another example to early fans of Weller's indebtedness to classic songwriting structures, he takes a dig at who would become the enemy in much of his work,

Who makes the rules that make people select,
Who is to judge that your ways are correct,
The media as watchdog is absolute shit,
The TV telling you what to think.

As Weller delivers the last line, Foxton destroys a TV with a single swift kick. (Subtlety wasn't a strong point with The Jam.) This middle eight also delivers the first swear word of a lyrical canon that is, as previously mentioned, pleasingly high on expletives. Indeed, for a band that eventually became so popular they were considered mainstream, the ability of Weller to drop 'unsuitable' words into singles that were played on prime-time radio is a wondrous thing. The song ends abruptly with one of Weller's favourite musical motifs, the guitar 'Morse-coding', across the pick-ups.

In the space of two minutes, The Jam introduced both themselves and some of the musical traits that became characteristic of the band in later years. It's only a pity the video was never more widely seen at the time as 'In The City' was chosen for the single. And if anyone can tell me why there's a shop mannequin made up to resemble a zombie lurking in the background, answers on a postcard to the address given at the end of the programme.

'I've Changed My Address' (Weller)
Not the most pleasant of subjects, running away from a persistent girlfriend by moving house doesn't seem the most gentlemanly or easiest way to end a relationship. But when you're 17 years old, it might seem the logical step. As the second verse comes in, Weller uses the language of the boxing ring to show just how confrontational he sees this marriage malarkey:

> Would've liked to explain first,
> But it was a split decision thing.

The track owes something to 'A Legal Matter' from The Who's debut album *My Generation*, unsurprising as the record was a constant source of inspiration for Weller and he'd taken it to his musical heart, explaining, 'I'd tried to write (*My Generation*) for our first album'. Musically, it's a little R&B, it's a little punk, it's very The Jam at this point. The lyrics don't show the protagonist in a particularly good light:

> No-one's gonna tie me down,
> No-one tell me what to do,
> Can't you see I've got to be free,
> Sorry baby that's the way it is with me.

It's a spiky number showing Weller's aggressive guitar style, but more than that, it gives us an insight into the way Foxton's bass playing progressed through the years. When there are only two melodic instruments in your band, both must play a full role, and through the years, Foxtons's running bass lines became an intrinsic part of The Jam's sound.

'Slow Down' (Williams)
Starting as they mean to go on, The Jam introduce the first recorded cover of a career that had a remarkably high number, and covers were something that the band kept falling back on until the very end. Surprisingly for a punk or new wave band, this cover of Larry Williams' 1958 R&B stomper is almost apologetically flat. Whereas Williams' recording starts with an explosion of sound, The Jam's feels leaden-footed. The track benefits from Foxton's insistent bass, showing the kind of muscle and fluidity that became his recognisable style, and Weller plays a classic R&B solo that is reminiscent of Elvis' guitarist Scotty Moore, until he adds a rather tired 'plectrum scratching down the E string' at the end in an attempt, presumably, to 'punk it up'. That

The Beatles also covered the track when playing at Liverpool's Cavern Club undoubtedly has something to do with The Jam choosing it for their set. In the end, it doesn't quite work and, in the end, the best thing the track has going for it is that it's not the worst cover on the album.

'I Got By In Time' (Weller)
'I Got By In Time' is the first song on the album where Weller sings as opposed to snarling like some punk caricature. Lyrically, it begins in standard boy-loses-girl territory, but the second verse shows Weller in a more emotionally open place as the words seem to point toward his one-time close friend and original Jam member, Steve Brookes:

> Saw a guy that I used to know,
> Man he'd changed so much.
> I think it hurt him to say 'hello',
> Cause he hardly opened his mouth.
> Yeah well he was my best friend a few years ago,
> We were truly inseparable.

That the song appears to have been written about someone he knew makes it something of a collector's item for The Jam, as many of Weller's subsequent songs were based on characters that came from his imagination. Lyrically, it also tells of Weller's infatuation with youth, and the possibilities that youth offers, whilst also admitting that the promise of youth is rarely fulfilled:

> We were young,
> We were full of ideals,
> We were gonna pull this whole world,
> But something happened,
> I didn't know why,
> But that's the way that it goes.

It's also a change musically from most of the album. Starting with tight snare rolls and single guitar chords and bass notes, it rolls along with pop punch – no startling solos or faux-Motown backing vocals – and tells its story in two minutes, the end of the song replicating the intro.

Essentially, 'I Got By In Time' is something of a throwaway song, but it gave insight into the way Weller moved in later years and his willingness to open himself up on song, something that he never did during his often flat, unhelpful TV and magazine interviews.

'Away From The Numbers' (Weller)
For many, the best song on the album, 'Away From The Numbers' was played live throughout the band's career and appears in a live format on various

B-sides and live albums. Weller has said the song took 'months to write' and, in comparison to the rest of the tunes on *In The City*, it's not hard to see why. Lyrically, Weller, even at 17 years old, writes in a state of introspection,

I was the type who knocked at old men,
Who together at tables sit and drink beer,
Then I saw that I was really the same,
So this link's breaking away from the chain.

It's an admirable wish and one shared by many of his contemporaries who, in 1976 and 1977, were forming bands at an exponential rate, and the single-minded belief The Jam had that they would amount to something is clear in the lyrics:

Away from the numbers,
Is where I'm gonna be.

Knowing how steeped in mod culture Weller was, it's impossible to think he didn't know that 'numbers' was the term the older, cooler mods of the 1960s used as a derogatory term for young wannabees who bought their clothes from Woolworths, the 'number' referring to the numbers printed on t-shirts in a copy of US Ivy League university clothes. Who are the numbers Weller is referring to? As he wrote the lyrics before the band had a record deal, he could be referring to his old mates left behind in Woking. Is he trying to say he's had enough of his peers, that perhaps he's better than they are?

And all those fools I thought were my friends,
They now stare at me and don't see a thing.

If so, he wouldn't be the first 17-year-old to think they're better than everyone else, and if you can't display naked bravado at that age, when can you? Of course, as Weller and, by extension, The Jam sought to differentiate themselves from the phalanx of punk bands with not only clothing but basic musical ability, by now, the numbers could refer to his punk contemporaries who were also eager to be noticed.

Power chords open the song, long and ringing and in relation to the choppy, aggressive playing of most of the album, it's almost ponderous, but there are some nice oohs and aahs that try to push the song along. The longish musical breaks between the verses ending and chorus kicking in mean that at just over four minutes, 'Away From The Numbers' is the longest song on the album. In fact, if you ignore the extended codas of 'The Eton Rifles', 'Precious' and 'In The Crowd', and take into account the recorded background noises of 'Tube Station', 'Away From The Numbers' is one of the longest album tracks Weller wrote when in The Jam. Proof it would seem that whatever the prevailing wind of speed and energy a good song finds its own pace and rhythm.

'Batman Theme' (Hefti)
When The Who released 'Batman' on their 1966 *Ready, Steady, Who* EP, it had at least some contemporary resonance as Adam West's tongue-in-cheek portrayal of the Caped Crusader was on British TV screens at the time. A decade later, and with no humour apparently visible (though perhaps the humour is meant to be intrinsic), The Jam tacked it on to the end of side one of *In The City*. At first, it seems mercifully short at one minute and three seconds, but then, for no reason, and somewhat cruelly, it kicks in again for another 22 seconds.

I've heard this called a 'live favourite' over the years, and it's certainly a blistering performance on record, and that's all well and good, but the idea of something being live, certainly in the days before a live show was watched through the screens of a thousand smartphones and uploaded to social media the second a song ended, was that it was in the moment and couldn't be recaptured. And that's where the 'Batman Theme' should have been left; in the moment, to be remembered or forgotten, whichever may be the case. File under; 'why bother'.

'In The City' (Weller)
7" cat. no. 2058 866.
UK release date: 29 April 1977
Highest UK chart placing: 40
Originally called 'In The City There's A Thousand Things I Wanna Say To You' because, Weller explained, 'even then I was into pretentious titles', the band's first single opens side two of the album.

Starting with a ferocious solo guitar riff (in one ear of your headphones), then joined by Foxton following the chord progression (in the other ear) and finally a frenetic tight snare roll from Buckler, the song attacks the senses and powers its way through the next two minutes 30 seconds without pausing for breath. The lyrics are the pained expression of someone railing against the old men who run our lives and now it's the chance for youth to have their time in the sun:

In the city there's a thousand faces all shining bright,
And those golden faces are under twenty-five.
They wanna say, they gonna tell ya,
About the young idea,
You better listen now you've said your bit.

Weller has said the band felt 'In The City' was so strong they would open a gig with it, play it in the middle, end the show with it and play it as an encore. That might be too much for any but a devoted fan, but it showed the depth of belief The Jam had in the song. A highest chart placing of 40 might have been disappointing, especially as the band performed it on their debut *Top Of The Pops* appearance – introduced by David 'Kid' Jensen as 'an effervescent new 45' – which was usually a dead cert for pushing a single up the charts, but it was certainly respectable for a band unknown to much of the UK. As the Sex Pistols were rapidly becoming persona non grata and The Clash had made clear their intention of not appearing on the nation's top music show, it left The Jam to fill the hole and their performance of 'In The City' was the first of any punk/new wave band on the programme.

What the single did do was impress the critics; though it gives mention to Weller's obvious influences, the *NME*'s Steve Clark wrote, 'the most convincing British-penned teenage anthem I've heard in a very long time'. Weller, writing in the first person, is voicing the impotence felt by his generation. Of course, those in charge will never listen to youth – though the power of social media is making inroads in that respect – but, in 1977, Weller can at least voice the opinion that 'If it don't work, at least we can say we tried'.

The video accompanying the release is a straightforward performance piece – with the band's amps and spare guitars on show telling us, 'Hey, look, we're a proper band' – set against backdrops of black and white photographs of urban, presumably London, scenes. If the words aren't enough, here are some pictures to help you along. The cover of the 7" is the sprayed band name logo and three black and white snapshots taken from a gig sellotaped to the tiled backdrop of the album cover. This cover was the first that many of the public would know of The Jam and it does its job simply but effectively; here's the band's name and here's what they look like. Weller and Foxton both sport Union Jack badges on the lapels of their suits and Foxton has a very impressive Elvis lip-curl. The back of the sleeve repeats the back of the album sleeve, though this time with a tight live band shot. If you look closely, you can make out some of the word 'skill' on Weller's amp. The phrase was 'Fire and Skill' and was used as the title to a Jam covers compilation album and a live album over a decade later.

I'll give the last word on the track to Steve Clark:

A huge hit and a record those narrow-minded reactionaries who control our radio would have to play.

'Sounds From The Street' (Weller)

The idea of trying to change what might be your place in society, and the role you might be expected to play in it, is tackled again in 'Sounds From The Street'. Musically, this was supposed to be a 'surf song', but as Weller admitted, the band 'didn't have the vocals', though that didn't stop them from giving it a go. For the second time on the album, Weller sings the words (as opposed to spitting them out) and there are surf-like oohs and aahs all over the place, which add to the general optimism that Weller is pushing:

Sounds from the city, sound so pretty,
Young bands playing,
Young kids digging,
And I dig them.

Most Jam fans will be aware that this is the song where Weller feels the need
to excuse The Jam's suburban upbringing:

I know I come from Woking,
And you'll say I'm a fraud,
But my heart is in the city where it belongs.

He acknowledges that the London he loves is not really him, but he's doing
his best to join in. It's a desperate belief that you can't be authentic unless
you're part of the big city scene and what would a kid from the suburbs
know about the struggles of life in the nation's capital? In some ways, the
song's lyrics have something of the schizophrenic about them. On the one
hand, Weller was desperate to be included in what punk was trying to
achieve but he's already acknowledging the desperation of the situation and
distancing himself from the punk credo of 'destroy', telling us that, whatever
the problems are with society, we must try to address them:

We're never gonna change a thing,
And the situation's rapidly decreasing.
But what can I do?
I'm trying to be true,
That's more than you,
At least I'm doing something.

'Non-Stop Dancing' (Weller)
'Non-Stop Dancing' was inspired by the northern soul all-nighters that
proliferated across 1970s Britain, and more specifically for Weller at the
Bisley Pavilion near Woking.

The song's structure is classic R&B, and another indication that The Jam
were never really punks; it suited them at the time to walk through the
musically stagnant door the Pistols had smashed to bits, though Weller was
undoubtedly smitten by the whole punk ethic. (In an interview Weller gave
during a tour to promote the *Setting Sons* album, he said, 'We didn't climb
aboard the (band) wagon; all of a sudden we were being quoted as a new
wave band'. I've always thought this was a tad disingenuous, as without punk
or new wave, it's difficult to see how The Jam would even have existed in the
form they took.

Unsurprisingly, lyrically, it never hits the heights. Weller was just 16 when
he wrote it, and 'non-stop groovin' baby, baby' was never likely to win an

27

Ivor Novello, but it rattles along engagingly enough and the sentiment in the
beautifully handled middle-eight hits home.

> People say we're wasting our time,
> They don't seem to understand,
> 'Cos when you're dancing all night long,
> It gives you the feeling that you belong.

Who, as a teenager, didn't want to belong?

'Time For Truth' (Weller)

Despite Weller saying in 1977, 'I don't want to get too involved in politics',
'Time For Truth' is certainly a political song, attacking the Labour government
of the day (though the soon-to-be Conservative government would add more
fuel to Weller's political fire) and the police, who had unleashed a wave of
protest over the alleged killing of a nightclub doorman whilst in custody and
the subsequent alleged cover-up:

> And you're trying to hide it from us,
> But you know what I mean,
> Bring forward those six pigs,
> We wanna see them swing so high.

(Calling for the capital punishment of police officers was something of a
one-off for a band who were resolutely pacifist in their intentions, despite
the sometimes confrontational and aggressive nature of their lyrics. Weller
never claimed to have the answers, he was just pointing out the problems,
though perhaps here he somewhat oversteps the mark.)

The song itself has a stop/start rhythm that gives space for the combative
lyrics aimed at then Labour Prime Minister James Callaghan ('Uncle
Jimmy'):

> Whatcha trying to say that you haven't tried to say before?
> You're just another red balloon with a lot of hot gas,
> Why don't ya fuck off?

And it's a heartfelt 'fuck off' at that. Although the general lyric attacks the
establishment, there's an awkward turn of events later in the song, which
was grist to the mill for the punk hierarchy who thought The Jam were 'little
Englanders' in their outlook. The Union flags that were part of The Jam's
stage set not helping in that matter, as Weller asks:

> Whatever happened to the great Empire?
> You bastards have turned it into manure.

Perhaps there's a dose of sarcasm running through the line, but it's difficult to detect. Weller appears to be defending the indefensible and later, with 'The Eton Rifles' and the artwork for *Setting Sons*, would take a more belligerent stance against Empire. Despite the confusing tone, when the dust has settled, 'Time For Truth' is one of the best tracks on the album and shows the band how they were at the time: young, uncompromising, a little bit naive, and desperate to have a voice.

'Takin' My Love' (Weller)
B-side to 'In The City'
A very early song, written with original band member Steve Brookes in 1973, 'Takin' My Love' was rearranged, and Brookes' name dropped from the credits. Weller, in a barked vocal delivery, manages to take what is essentially a love song and turn it into a 100mph debauched scream. Replace The Jam with a swingin' rhythm and blues orchestra, Weller with Big Joe Turner and put the brakes on, and 'Takin' My Love' could be a mid-50s rock and roll rave of a tune.

> Well come on pretty baby you know what I like now,
> You're shakin' all over and it's feeling alright now,
> You're rockin' and rollin' and I don't know what to say,
> But daddy's little cat's gonna rock all day.

Though one of the later lines, 'We'll go fuck around 2 am' probably wouldn't have made it to the final edit in the 1950s. In all honesty, if the band had more material, it should never have made it onto the album. It ticks the album's generic musical boxes of fast, frenetic and not much over two minutes but does little else.

'Bricks And Mortar' (Weller)
The album's closer again touches on politics, or perhaps social commentary would be a better description, as Weller questions the desire for modernism at the cost of human misery:

> This is progress,
> Nothing stands in its path.

The song also has a personal angle when Weller sings:

> While hundreds are homeless,
> They're constructing a parking space.

Weller's own childhood home in Woking had been bulldozed in the name of the aforementioned progress.

Along similar lines as 'Time For Truth's name-checking of the then British PM, the tune highlights how, when you're singing about contemporary subjects, lyrics will inevitably become dated over time, and asking why 'a man whose house has cost 40 grand' has a right to make decisions about inner city planning has lost some of its weight. £40,000 wouldn't buy you much of a house in modern-day London, or in modern-day anywhere in the UK for that matter.

The song itself is medium-paced – despite Buckler pushing it along with a four-to-the-floor drum pattern – and as such has a maudlin 'the battle has been lost' vibe, but musically, it does show how Weller's own style of simultaneous rhythm and lead guitar playing was beginning to take shape and which would in time become an intrinsic part of the band's sound. The last third of the track, and the closing of the album, descends into the type of feedback The Who would be proud of and further shows the band's 1960s credentials but also highlights just what a racket The Jam could make.

'All Around The World' (Weller)

7" cat. no. 2058 903.
Recorded at Stratford Place Studios, London
Produced by Chris Parry and Vic Smith
UK release date: 8 July 1977
Highest UK chart placing: 13
Opening with a drilled snare roll, bass drum count in and power chords, 'All Around The World' doesn't have the riff of 'In The City', but I think it's the better song. More focused (really), more energetic (yes, really) and more optimistic, it pointedly has a go at the Pistols' anarchy message:

What's the point in saying destroy?
We want a new life for everyone.

It's also much easier for a fledgling guitar player to get his head around, the verse being a simple A-G. I know this because I bought *The Jam Songbook*, a slim volume that introduces us to some of Dave Waller's poetry and includes a verse that reappeared on the band's next album. (The book also tells us 'All Around The World' was arranged for the book, not the album, by Ziggy Ludvigsen. He's a hard man to pin down is Ziggy, but the internet tells us he played saxophone in Camden pub jazz jams in the 1960s and 70s and was credited as the arranger of a Pink Floyd songbook. Strange.)

As the song hits its stride, and the track doesn't last long, two minutes 30 seconds or thereabouts, Weller makes it clear what he's looking for:

All over the country (We want a new direction)
I said all over this land (We need a reaction)
Well there should be a youth explosion (Inflate creation)

These words, 'direction', 'reaction' and 'creation', are repeated throughout the song and if that wasn't enough to show how important they were to Weller, they're printed on the rear of the single's picture sleeve. (The Jam rarely left anything to chance when trying to get their message across.) Later, *Direction, Reaction, Creation* became the title of the band's retrospective 5 CD box set released in 1997.

As mentioned in the book's introduction, the band played the single live on Marc Bolan's new TV show, *Marc*. After Bolan introduces 'Jam', the band lay into a throbbing explosion of a performance. As the song comes to a close and Buckler starts his snare rolls, we see a drumstick fly off out of shot and the track duly stumbles to an ignominious end, Weller and Foxton unsure as to what has just happened, Buckler giving a shrug of the shoulders. Live telly, eh! To me, what's important about this performance was not only that The Jam were clearly the first act to be invited to play on the show (Bolan's introduction makes it obvious), something of a coup in itself, but that it was a prime-time music show and the bands played live. With little more than Jools Holland's increasingly unwatchable *Later...* to provide live music on 'normal' telly, we have to thank the proliferation of punk bands at the time that forced TV producers to give the untapped youth market the artists they wanted to see.

The front of the single's sleeve shows the band in their now trademark black suits, and 'Jam shoes' so scruffy a modern stylist wouldn't be able to sleep at night. The 'Jam' logo is again spray painted, but this time, on what appears to be a backdrop made from a yellow stretched plastic sheet. Alongside the usual credited suspects of song producer(s), sleeve designer (Bill Smith again) and photographer (Martyn Goddard again), we're informed 'hair: schumi'. How many new wave bands credited their hairdresser on a picture sleeve? The photos do have something of a catalogue model feel to them, Weller's dogtooth check jacket casually slung over a shoulder whilst wearing something akin to a pink dinner shirt. Maybe it *was* all about the fashion?

Of course, it wasn't (all) about fashion: The Jam were about the excitement of youth, and what the future could hold despite the obstacles laid in the path of a generation who thought their time had come. Although every generation before and after thinks much the same, and Weller would become more worldly-wise and cynical in time, this two-minute belter, with Weller's guitar tricks of scratched guitar strings and 'Morse-coding', is present and correct. 'All Around The World' had them knocking on the door of the Top Ten, though it would take them another year, and a lot of heartache before they managed the feat.

'Carnaby Street' (Foxton)
B-side to 'All Around The World'
Foxton's first songwriting credit, on which he takes the lead vocal, is a lament at the demise of London's mod fashion hub of the 1960s. The lyrics are full

of the kind of imagery that had the band earmarked as Tories and too British for their own good:

> The street is a mirror for our country,
> Reflects the rise and fall of our nation.
> The street that was a legend is a mockery,
> A part of the British tradition, gone down the drain.

At one point, Foxton attests Carnaby Street, 'Was a part of the British monarchy'. The more you look at the lyrics, the dodgier they become. Coupled with Weller's statement in an *NME* interview from 7 May 1977, 'We think we'll vote Conservative at the election', which was aimed at annoying the punk elite rather than a genuine belief in the Tory manifesto, Foxton's words were easy pickings for critics of the band. It didn't help that The Jam were still draping Union Jacks over their equipment at gigs, and that, along with the rise in the public mind of the violent, right-wing National Front, put The Jam in an awkward position. In fact, for much of The Jam's career, violence was never far away when it came to the live shows, something I can attest to personally having run the gauntlet of skinheads at Jam gigs more than once. It was something the band could never understand as they preached unity and the need for young people to stick together, but however much Weller tried, the kids just wouldn't listen.

As for the track, the best thing for everyone is to draw a line under it and move on.

Standards Rule OK – This Is The Modern World To News Of The World

This Is The Modern World

LP cat. no. 2383 475
Recorded at Basing Street Studios, London
Produced by Chris Parry and Vic Smith
UK release date: 18 November 1977
Highest UK chart placing: 22

It's a truism in the music industry that for an 'organic' band, by which I mean one that has formed over time through personal friendships or meeting friends of friends with similar musical tastes, and not conceived in a petri dish by a production or management company, their first album can take two, three, four years or longer to write. The songs of a debut album, as we've seen with *In The City*, are brought to rehearsal spaces, discussed, picked apart, arranged and rearranged and played live across countless shows until, eventually, you have the finished article. Over these first years, the band find their feet, and if their luck is in, they sign a record deal and release an album. [In 1977, it was mainly record deals with established companies that paved the way to having a career, though punk and the DIY ethic did their best to change that.] The debut album is made up of a dozen or so songs that have been honed over time to the band's satisfaction. If they're lucky and good enough, the album enjoys a modicum of success and the record company comes calling, saying they need another album pronto, preferably written, recorded and ready to go within a year. And this is where we begin with *This Is The Modern World*.

Released a few days shy of six months after the band's debut hit the shops – the band's A&R man, Chris Parry, said he thought 'momentum was important' – *Modern World* is a hotch-potch of ideas lacking in clarity and cohesion. Having said that, being released so close to *In The City*, the band could have been forgiven for settling for a similar-sounding album, two-minute blasts of thrashing guitars, that they attempted something different shows at this early stage, their desire to keep moving forward musically.

Weller, never the most prolific of songwriters, had hit something of a fallow period even for him and this was exacerbated by his falling in love with Gill Price (who later appeared as the model on the cover of the 'Beat Surrender' single). As any 19-year-old might, he spent more and more of his time with Price and less with the group. Weller, Foxton and Buckler were never the best of friends, but they had a common goal; to make The Jam successful, a goal which, to that point, was Weller's only focus and drive in life, but Weller was losing interest in the band. That they were across the Atlantic pushing their British way of life on the Americans didn't help matters. An American magazine advertisement, across a photo of The Jam, was worded: 'These three British subjects are the illegitimate offspring of Peter Townshend, Ray Davies, Keith Richard, John Lennon and Jimmy Page', and in the corner, above the Polydor label, 'We bring England closer to home'. I'm not sure if even I'd have bought into that. And who calls Pete Townshend, 'Peter'?

The pressure from Polydor for new material was increasing. To try to fire their creative energy, the band booked themselves into a rehearsal studio in the countryside but, as Foxton remembered, it didn't work.

We'd try and bash a load of half-baked songs into shape, the idea being that because we were in the middle of nowhere, we wouldn't have fuck all to do and be very productive. We just finished up going down the pub every day.

Old ideas were rehashed, and Foxton took responsibility for some of the songwriting. Later, Foxton would have his day in the sun, but this album isn't it. It would be harsh to single out his songs among weak efforts from Weller, but the band's subsequent career clearly shows that without Weller's songwriting, The Jam wouldn't have been anywhere near the band they became. Having said that, without the contributions of Foxton and Buckler, The Jam wouldn't have been anywhere near the band they became. With 20/20 hindsight, *Modern World* can easily be read as an obvious bridge between *In The City* and *All Mod Cons*, with some of the fire of the former and some of the social observations of the latter, and there are some nice musical ideas, but the critics were divided. Chris Brazier in *Melody Maker*:

The production...is well on the thin side...(the songs) are all adequate but thoroughly ordinary and don't represent any development (and) some of the songs are lyrically weak.

The *NME*'s Mick Farron also piled in:

Some of the riffs don't stand up to the amount of repetition that they are subjected to, and that after a couple of tracks, the vocals do lean towards the monotonous.

On the other side of the divide was Barry Cain in the *Record Mirror*:

This Is The Modern World reflects a definite PROGRESSION, a definite identity mould...here Weller is making an obvious attempt at creating a Jam SOUND. He succeeds. Brilliantly.

Barry Cain was already friends with the band and stayed friends with them for the rest of The Jam's career, garnering a namecheck on the back of the *Modern World* album. Weller used a quote from a gig review that Cain had written about a show at the Royal Academy of Art, as a lyric in 'Life From A Window'. As Cain remembered:

> I alluded to the colours of the Union Jack (being used as a backdrop), taking you through the three moods that you get at a Jam concert. Red hot, expanding to white heat, contracting to teenage blue.

Decades later, during an episode of *PaulWellerFanPodcast.Com*, Cain admitted, 'I'd always give them a 5-star review', so perhaps his opinion requires a large handful of salt.

Still, on the positive side of the fence, Chas De Walley in *Sounds* stated that '(*Modern World*) is one of the best albums I've heard in a long time'. Which, without wanting to sound too flippant, begs the question; what was Chas listening to at the time?

To carry on the theme of the album sounding 'thin', I think the same observation could be made for the album's artwork. Polydor art director Bill Smith was back on the case and this time he got the gritty urban (there's that word again) landscape he'd hoped for with *In The City*. The band posed beneath a flyover with two brutalist tower blocks dominating the background. Weller has swapped his Damned badge for a Who badge, though it appears Buckler is now wearing Weller's cast-off alongside a Union Jack badge. Weller wears a white jumper that has two arrows made from gaffer tape stuck to the front of it in the style of Roger Daltrey (the arrow had become something of a mod staple since The Who first used it in their original band logo). Buckler and Foxton stare into the middle distance whilst Weller glowers at the camera. It's all a bit cliched. Perhaps the most startling part of the image for a modern young viewer is that Buckler is holding a lit cigarette. On the front of an album sleeve!

The rear of the sleeve is a perfunctory live shot, Weller arching his back mid-solo in front of his Vox AC30 amps and Foxton in mid-leap with the Jam logo as a backdrop. As I've said, it all seems a bit 'thin', a bit 'who cares?' The inside sleeve, with lyrics provided (something that became a constant for subsequent Jam albums, and a boon for the young teenage fan desperate to soak in every word that Weller might utter), has a series of illustrations credited to Conny Jude that reflect some of the lyrical content of the album. It's a singular collection of pictures ranging from the touching to the grotesque to the, in the case of the boy in the wheelchair, borderline offensive. But they add some guts to the package.

'The Modern World' (Weller)
7" cat. no. 2058 945
Recorded at Basing Street Studios, London
Produced by Chris Parry and Vic Smith
UK release date 21 October 1977
Highest UK chart placing: 36

The album begins, much like its predecessor, with solo guitar power chords but where 'Art School' was urgent and frenetic, 'Modern World' takes a slightly more measured pace. Still tight and punchy, the song is propelled by Foxton and Buckler, though Weller's delivery lacks energy. The track had been recorded before *In The City* had been released and was aired on John Peel's BBC Radio One show before the debut album hit the shops, so it was a surprise to many that it wasn't on *In The City*. The fact it was saved as the second album's opener was, in hindsight, a good move as it's one of the stronger tracks on an unremarkable record.

From the beginning, Weller is on the attack lyrically:

What kind of a fool do you think I am?
You think I know nothing of the modern world.

And his belief in himself and The Jam is apparent despite the fact the single had been written prior to a record deal:

I've learnt more than you'll ever know,
Even at school I felt quite sure,
That one day I would be on top,
And I'd look down upon the map,
The teachers who said I'd be nothing.

That it was a testing time for the band is not in any doubt; fallings out with their musical contemporaries, a struggle to come up with new songs and a spiky relationship with the music press, but Weller has a clear message for the doubters, with 'I don't give two fucks about your review'.

Disappointingly, though wholly understandably, the 7" single has the more radio-friendly, 'I don't give a damn about your review'. It was an obvious change to make, and the band made another appearance on *Top Of The Pops* (Weller's Rickenbacker had the words 'I am nobody' written across the front if there were any questions about his state of mind at the time). 'Modern World' stalled at number 36 in the chart, a huge comedown after 'All Around The World', and a precursor to the testing times that were to follow over the next 12 months.

As for the sleeve of the 7", it's a shot taken from the *In The City* sessions but has been toyed around with in an attempt to make it look 'different'. As with the album artwork, and to an extent the album itself, it's a half-arsed attempt.

'London Traffic' (Foxton)
The worst track on the album. Fifth-form poetry trying so hard to get the words to rhyme, that any subtlety or originality has no hope of finding space:

Drive round London in a car,
Don't really want to go far,
So many cars fill the streets,
Wonder why we bother at all.

And it doesn't get any better:

London traffic is a problem,
London traffic too many cars.

Musically, however, there are redeeming features in the harmonies, which deserve better and, indeed, are used to better effect on other tracks and the driving (pardon the pun) guitars give the track some gusto. In fairness to Foxton, he had stepped up when the Weller well had run dry.

Polydor had played with the idea of releasing a live album, and a set at London's 100 Club had been recorded for the purpose as the band's live performances were so strong, but the label changed their minds as Weller and Foxton between them brought enough new material for the *Modern World* sessions. Whether the material was actually any good is a moot point, though there are genuinely great moments, you just have to look for them.

At the end of 'London Traffic', we hear a car door slamming and the screech of tyres as the car speeds away. I can't blame the driver.

'Standards' (Weller)

Touring up and down the country for weeks and months on end gives you time to indulge in other activities, though, in the time before the internet, not many, and reading books was one of them. It was around this time that Weller discovered, among others, George Orwell and the author's *1984*. Written in 1948, the novel tells the story of Winston Smith, living in a totalitarian regime, always at war with someone or other, the combatants changing as often as the weather, and which alters the truth to fit the state's perspective. Winston himself works at the records department of the Ministry of Truth, rewording old newspaper articles to match the current party line, and Weller reminds us that the regime is all:

We have the power to control the whole land,
You never must question our motives or plans.

Musically, it steals openly from The Who's 1965 debut 'I Can't Explain' with its chopped single guitar chords and is what might be called standard Jam fare (no more puns, I promise). Lyrically, however, it shows Weller continuing to grow as a songwriter who has something to say and is discovering new ways to say it. Rather than the more usual 'I' to make

comments about 'you' and 'them', 'Standards' takes the voice of the
state, 'we', and gives us the story from their perspective. Of course, their
perspective is arrogant ...

> 'Cos we'll outlaw your voices, do anything we want,
> We've nothing to fear from the nation.

...and threatening, as Weller reminds us of the fate of *1984*'s protagonist,

> Look, you know what happened to Winston.

The song ends with a repeated chant as the state drills into us what is best
for us, 'Standards rule, OK'. If you're in any doubt as to the rights and
wrongs of the state's actions, it's best not to question too closely, after all,
ignorance is strength.

'Life From A Window' (Weller)

As a song, 'Life From A Window' is just another album track, though in
that respect it's not alone. On future albums, Jam songs would stand out as
individual masterpieces or important cogs in the flow of the record, *Modern
World* is more a collection of standalone pieces of music.

Before the song starts rolling, we hear the thump of a bass string, a
nonchalant guitar chord, Weller asking Foxton if his bass line is ready and,
not for the first time or last time, Weller's '1, 2, 3, 4' introduction. If this
was a diversionary tactic to convince the listener that the band recorded
their tracks 'live', the conceit is pulled apart from the opening chord where
acoustic guitar, employed for the first time on a Jam recording, is overdubbed
with electric guitar. Even for Weller, whose guitar playing was becoming
more and more adept, that would be a step too far.

The simplicity of the track lends it a degree of charm, but lyrically, it shows
little of Weller's depth and foresight, except perhaps for the middle-eight,
where we catch a glimpse of what was to come on the following album,
All Mod Cons, with an acerbic comment on what I always took to be the
shallowness of the record industry and its 'we're with you all the way, until
we're not' attitude to bands and musicians.

> Some people that you see around you.
> Tell you how devoted they are.
> They tell you something new on Sunday, but come Monday
> They've changed their minds.

The song tumbles to an end with chiming chords, solid bass notes and
punchy drum rolls. It's a pop song, done pretty well, but it is just another
song.

'The Combine' (Weller)

Alongside Orwell, Weller was also reading Ken Kesey's *One Flew Over The Cuckoo's Nest*, a tale of a sane man locked away in a psychiatric institution, and another tale of totalitarianism. One of the institution's inmates, a Native American called Chief Bromden, calls society 'The Combine', there to oppress the people, and the ward where the novel is set is where the people are 'fixed' to become model citizens. Lyrically, Weller comes in halfway through a thought:

> And life is very difficult when you're in a crowd.
> When you're in the crowd, you see things as they really are,
> You can smell the fear and hate, generated by all around.

(It's a sentiment that didn't last long for Weller as in the following years' *All Mod Cons,* he opens a song, 'When I'm in the crowd, I don't see anything', but who knew exactly what they were talking about when they were 19 years old? I'm not always sure what I'm talking about now that I'm 58.)

In the end, the song doesn't add up to much lyrically or musically, though the end changes tack nicely and the lyric explains the sort of opiate that society, or The Combine, are offered to keep them pliant. As already mentioned, however, when writing of contemporary things, the connection can quickly be lost to today's younger listener and so we have 'Ena Sharples' and 'Page 3 girls', and mentioning the 'war in Rhodesia', a country that no longer exists except in its current form of Zimbabwe. These kinds of specifics set a song in a place and time, but Weller was at his most perceptive when storytelling and focusing on timeless issues, such as matters within society that affect us all, which today are pretty much the same as they were then; plus ça change, and all that.

'Don't Tell Them You're Sane' (Foxton)

As Weller had been struggling to come up with new material for *Modern World*, with the 'difficult second album' problem kicking in, Foxton stepped up and brought along some new songs. 'Don't Tell Them You're Sane' starts encouragingly enough with a short, twisting bassline, which the guitar follows note for note, but then the drums kick in, lumpy and predictable, and the melody line moves from being slick to clumsy in the space of a line, 'Looks like he's forgotten, but is he?' and is followed by a lumbering riff taking us into verse two.

Another track that takes inspiration from Kesey's *One Flew Over The Cuckoo's Nest*, it tells the story of a boy locked away in an asylum who nevertheless believes in his own sanity, it's the warders who are the ones at fault:

> His mind it ticks more than you know,
> One day something in his head will click.

39

Warders fill him full of lies, he fights, he knows,
They'll never convince him that he's mad.

The problem comes when Foxton, who shows admirable sympathy for his subject (indeed Foxton, unlike Weller, often shows sympathy for his subjects when writing about individuals) keeps ramming home the story, which is already so recognisable that at times it becomes lyrically redundant, 'Don't tell them you're sane, *but you are*'.

Though not the worst song on the album (just), at three minutes 40 seconds, it is the longest song. Foxton did have a tendency to make his tunes last longer than they should have simply by adding verses with repeated lyrics, something a more forceful producer might have nipped in the bud, but musically it has some nice touches; Weller's high oohs, and the sort of change in direction mid-song that pointed towards future Jam tunes.

'In The Street Today' (Weller)
Opening side two is a song that would have made more sense on the band's debut. 'In The Street Today' is a brash one minute 31 seconds; a pounding drum intro, R&B solo and three-chord pile-up highlighting the violence on Britain's streets. Weller borrowed one of the verses from his old Jam bandmate, Dave Waller, who was gaining some recognition for the poetry he'd left The Jam to pursue:

Murder on the terraces,
And fools in high places,
It's all so sickening,
And we're so satisfied.

And that's it.

'London Girl' (Weller)
Written in May 1977, it might have been included on the band's debut album but instead made its way onto *Modern World*. It's a well-worn tale of kids from the suburbs and beyond, drawn to the lights of the capital and finding that life isn't as sweet-smelling as it might seem in the boring shires.

Musically and lyrically, it's one of the duller offerings on the album, three verses pointing out the folly of the girl's desire for something, anything, that she can't find at home but will find in London:

Do you know what you're looking for?
Streets of gold, fame and fortune?

And so it goes on; sleeping on Waterloo Station before moving on to a 'posher squat' and wondering 'where your next meal will come from' but, worryingly, 'still it's better than living at home'. 'London Girl' paints a bleak picture of what life in London has to offer.

There's a musical and lyrical twist in the tale, however, and Foxton takes over the vocal line, offering a deal of empathy for the desperate protagonist:

I don't condemn what you've done,
I know what it is to be young,
You're only searching for today,
To seek the answers about yesterday,
And I hope you find...

The track stumbles to a close with power chords backed by bass and cymbal crashes, which I've always thought gives the song something of a pompous ending.

'I Need You (For Someone)' (Weller)

About as far away from the sloganeering of punk as it's possible to get, the lyrics are an open reflection of the emotions Weller was feeling at the time with his new girlfriend. This kind of openness isn't easy for someone who was, by his own admission, something of a shy loner despite the fact he was fast gaining a reputation within the media as surly, humourless and difficult to deal with. The pressure Weller, and the band, were under during the recording of *Modern World* needed an outlet and for Weller at least, he'd found someone to help him both keep his head together and who could be the calming voice of reason.

I need you to keep me straight,
When the world don't seem so great
And it's hard enough you know.
I need you to turn me off,
When you think I've said enough,
To the extent of being a bore.

Opening with power chords and rolling drums, underscored by Foxton's gentle oohs, it turns into a duet, as a surprising number of Jam songs do. There's no searing solo; the tune pushes along with a yearning and longing and plea to this new love,

Say you'll stay,
Make my day.

'I Need You' is another love song on an album that, given what The Jam were known for and best at, is overloaded with them. Too much sentimentality, too many medium-paced fillers and too little for the listener to get their teeth into.

'Here Comes The Weekend' (Weller)

With a title cribbed from the 1960s pop show *Ready, Steady Go!* and their by-line 'The Weekend Starts Here', the song begins with yet more power chords and Weller's spoken introduction, 'OK, alright, here it comes', sounding more like a warning of doom than an optimistic call for hedonism and the song doesn't lighten up,

> If we tell you that you've got two days to live,
> Then don't complain 'cos that's one more than you'd get in Zaire.

That might well be the case, but The Jam's audience weren't living in an African one-party totalitarian military dictatorship – at least, I'd guess, not many – so this heavy-handed warning is a bit off the mark.

'Weekend' is a straight-forward song addressed to those who worked all week with little to look forward to except the coming opportunity to get wasted, and at times, the lyrics are plain dull:

> So don't hang around and be foolish,
> Do something constructive with your weekend.

It's a scene played out in millions of homes and thousands of flats across Britain and even for those of us too young to be caught in the life loop of work, play, work, play, we had mothers and fathers who could relate to the lyrics in some way, it's not only young school leavers with jobs that go nowhere and whose only chance of fun is at the weekends.

> From Monday morning, I work for Friday night,
> Collect my wages and try to paint on the smell of soap.

At least among the depression of being caught in the rat race, there's some positivity, something to aim for, however short. At least there's another weekend just around the corner.

And then this happens:

> Eggs, eggs, eggs,
> Poached boiled or fried,
> They're good for the old,
> (Raspberry sound),
> Oh, shut up!

Spoken in a squeezed southern accent over a single electric guitar, tremolo to the fore, It could be a nod to The Who's 1967 album *Sell Out,* which interspersed the tracks with real and fake radio jingles for real and fake goods. The voice on The Who's album, which asks, 'What's for tea daughter'

(Heinz baked beans, in case you were wondering) is vaguely similar to the voice used by The Jam. I guess it was meant to be funny. But it isn't. Let's move on.

'Tonight At Noon' (Weller, Henri)
With a writing co-credit to 1960s Liverpool poet Adrian Henri, who provided the song's title from his own, same-titled poem, and provided the opening lines from his poem *In The Midnight Hour*:

> When we meet in the midnight hour…
> I will bring you night flowers coloured like your eyes.

[*In The Midnight Hour,* here isn't to be confused with the soul standard and *Modern World* closing track]. 'Tonight At Noon' is another medium-paced out-and-out love song, and the words, if not actually crooned, are softly delivered with unashamed warmth.

The tune opens with an acoustic riff, the first time a Jam track had opened in such a melancholy way, before rolling drums introduce the bass and we're off into 'city squares in winter rain' and 'walking down muddy lanes or empty streets' before ending with the best harmonies Weller and Foxton had delivered so far. If anyone thought of Weller as a one-dimensional battering ram of punk-fuelled rage, 'Tonight At Noon', along with others on the album, showed there was a more emotionally thoughtful side to his writing.

> Tonight at noon, I'll touch your hand,
> Held for a moment amongst strangers,
> Amongst the dripping trees,
> Country Girl.

While researching this book, I came across footage from a European concert, and it's quite the surprise. The film shows the band playing 'Tonight at Noon', Weller sporting a bright red 12-string Vox Tear Drop guitar. I'd never seen Weller play this guitar before or since, and never seen it in photos, be they live or promo shots. But the performance is heart-achingly tender, at a time when they were still wearing matching suits (grey in this instance) and still with the Union Jack draped across Weller's amp, and where most of the set would be at a furious pace.

'In The Midnight Hour' (Pickett, Cropper)
Staying with the very mod idea of cover versions on your album releases, the band chose to go full-on mainstream with perhaps one of the best-known soul tunes. Wilson Pickett's 'In The Midnight Hour' was released on the Stax label in 1965 and has since been covered by far too many artists to

mention. That The Jam decided to end their second album with it points to both a lack of material and imagination. Musically, it's what you might have expected if you'd heard *In The City* or been to any of the band's gigs, an attempt to beat each other to the end of the song, though a harmonica blast from Weller adds another layer before winding up proceedings. Whether he was channelling John Lennon or Lee Brilleaux with his mouth-organ solo has never been noted, but aside from that, it's a straight cover with no great changes to the melody or arrangement, just put your foot down and go for it. A disappointing end to a disappointing album.

'Sweet Soul Music' (Conley), 'Back In My Arms Again' (Holland, Dozier, Holland), 'Bricks And Mortar' (Weller)
B-side to 'The Modern World'
Recorded live at the 100 Club in London, these are songs that might have been part of the band's second album if Polydor hadn't had the good sense to realise what a mistake a live album would have been, although the idea had been fought by The Jam from the outset. 'Sweet Soul Music', Arthur Conley's 1967 love affair to the big soulsters of the day, swings with syncopation and a horn riff straight from a Western soundtrack, The Jam speed it up beyond what is sensible. Weller's breathless vocals are so unintelligible that the praise of Lou Rawls, Otis Redding, Wilson Pickett and James Brown goes largely unnoticed.

Slightly more respectful is the version of The Supremes' 'Back In My Arms Again', but still, in the maelstrom of 1977, everything had to be pumped up and the soulful yearning of Diana Ross is defeated by the bark of Weller. Most unsatisfactory of all is the 40 seconds of 'Bricks And Mortar' at the end of the side, where the song fades out before it's had a chance to get going. It might be pushing a metaphor too far, but the laziness of not taking the trouble to edit the song out when it would have been easy to do so, and, bearing in mind that 'The Modern World' single was released before the album, could be seen as a precursor to the underwhelming record that was to follow. No one seems all that bothered.

'News Of The World' (Foxton)
7" cat. no. 2058 995
Recorded at Basing Street Studios, London
Produced by Vic Smith and Chris Parry
UK release date: 24 February 1978
Highest UK chart placing: 27
Coming straight in with a nippy descending chord sequence, the opening of 'News Of The World' promises much and, for the most part, delivers. Although Weller begins the track with a spoken, and heavily echoed 'Punk rock, power pop', which seems to have little to do with the message of the song and more that Weller is stating his musical influences, or perhaps more

accurately at this point, what he'd fallen out with, this is Foxton's first outing as lead vocal on the A-side of a single and it was his best song to date.

Named from the now long defunct, and not at all mourned, Sunday tabloid, it's an open attack on the lies printed in the name of open journalism as Foxton warns, 'Don't believe in everything you see or hear'. Musically, it's as adept as anything the band had come up with to then and Weller performs an excellent R&B guitar break as the song flies along at pace. But the lyrics don't come up to scratch and some, it seems to me, were dated and patently untrue even then:

Look at the pictures taken by the cameras; they cannot lie.
The truth is in what you see, not what you read.

Though the middle-eight nails it in a pithy, simple way:

Never doubt,
Never ask,
Never moan.
Never search,
Never find,
Never know.

The observation is as true today as it was in 1978, perhaps more so with the polarisation of politics and the rampant, unceasing influence of social media.

Despite it charting higher than both 'In The City' and 'The Modern World', there was a tacit belief that the band could do better when Weller admitted that it was 'the best thing we had until we got into writing *All Mod Cons*'.

When the single was released, The Jam were on a five-week tour of America opening for US AOR band Blue Oyster Cult, which meant a video was needed. For reasons unexplained, the group dragged their kit to the roof of Battersea power station and dutifully mimed along in perfunctory fashion. The picture sleeve to the single, the photo again by Martyn Goddard, shows them strolling down Carnaby Street, more of a nod to the B-side of 'All Around The World', but though Weller and Foxton are in suits, button-down shirts and very noticeable Jam shoes, Buckler is wavering between mod (a target t-shirt) and rocker (a black leather biker's jacket). I think it's fair comment that Buckler wore the clothes to fit the band's image rather than his character. In a piece from the *Melody Maker* factfinders series, dated 11 June 1977, along with questions about parentage, siblings, where they live (all three say with their parents in Woking) and what kind of musical tuition they had (all three say 'self-taught'), when it comes to musical influences, favourite albums, musicians, singers and the like, Weller and Foxton are pretty uniform citing Motown, The Beatles, The Who, Otis Redding, Stevie Wonder and so on. Buckler's favourite single is 'Stayed Awake All Night' by Canadian rockers

Bachman-Turner Overdrive (arguably best known in the UK for the single 'You Ain't Seen Nothing Yet') and his favourite singer is Frank Sinatra. Not a mod, then.

It was Buckler who, when commenting on the photo shoot for the sleeve, said that 'some of the band' had been in the pub and were feeling a little worse for wear. Take a look at Foxton and you'll see what he means. For continuity's sake, the graffiti Jam logo is in situ, though nowhere near as prominently as in their previous single releases. It's an indication that The Jam were slowly, but ever so surely, becoming more recognisable. The sleeve also gives Weller a design credit, alongside Bill Smith, and shows that Weller took an interest in how the band were packaged from early in their career.

In 2005, the BBC's 'satirical' news show *Mock The Week* chose 'News Of The World' for its opening titles and, as it continued to be broadcast until October 2022, at least meant Foxton's bank account ticked over with royalty payments.

'Aunties And Uncles (Impulsive Youths)' (Weller)
B-side to 'News Of The World'
A person can write many things about Jam songs, but 'polite' isn't a word that might immediately spring to mind. Here, however, it's the first word I think of. Gone is the 'punk' vocal delivery, the accusatory lyrics and, it must be said, the excitement. 'Aunties And Uncles' is a song with leather patches on its cardigan, slippers on its feet and a cup of tea before an open fire. It begins intriguingly enough with a scratched, slightly off-kilter guitar and bass intro but soon settles into a medium-paced non-entity, which Weller tries to salvage with a forced vocal line, but it doesn't quite work.

Lyrically, there's little to get your teeth into other than a nice observation that:

The people around me,
Are looking for something,
But I've become blind 'cause I've found what I'm looking for.

That's not entirely true, as Weller spent his entire Jam career looking for the next thing, the next musical or lyrical idea, but sometimes it's OK to feel settled, if only for a short while.

There are some nice 'oohs' here and there, but they are so low down in the mix you can barely hear them. Perhaps purposely so, as they're a direct rip-off from the opening 'oohs' on The Who's 'Pictures of Lily'.

'Innocent Man' (Foxton)
B-side to 'News of The World'
Carrying on the petty larceny against The Who, 'Innocent Man' opens with an acoustic take on the power chords that introduce 'Baba O'Reilly' from

the 1971 *Who's Next* album and ends with a piano echoing the same chords. The piano was credited to Weller and it was the first time that any fan had an inkling that he was more than a guitar slinger (the frantic harmonica on 'Midnight Hour' notwithstanding).

The song tackles a worthy subject, capital punishment, and Foxton is clearly heartfelt in his delivery:

Well, what has he done to you or someone?
Nobody speaks or should he know?
Thinks they're all to blame, nothing clear to him anymore,
Can't think straight, can't sort himself out.

Unfortunately, the song suffers from Foxton's weaknesses as a songwriter, the obvious lyric:

The time has come,
For that man to be hung,
I hope you're convinced,
That he was the one.

And at almost four minutes, it outstays its welcome. Any value the song might have had, as far as pushing its intentions to the public is concerned, is lost as the second track on a B-side. Once again, as in many of the songs on *Modern World*, there are surf-style harmonies to see us to the end of the track, but The Jam were mining the same old seam, and it was quickly running dry. Something had to give.

To Be Someone Must Be A Wonderful Thing – All Mod Cons To When You're Young

All Mod Cons

LP cat. no. POLD 5008
Recorded at RAK Studios, London
Produced by Vic Coppersmith-Heaven
UK release date: 3 November 1978
Highest UK chart placing: 6

If Weller had always worn his mod credentials on his sleeve, this is where he turned them into a three-piece mohair suit complete with jacket with side vents five inches long.

For the first time, the design of the album is credited to Bill Smith and The Jam and Weller's influence is clear. From the title, which Weller admitted in the 2000 documentary, *The Making of All Mod Cons*, was partly so he could use the word 'mod'; to the font used on the front of the album, stolen from Andrew Oldham's Immediate record label, home to the Small Faces in the latter part of their career; to the Vespa schematic on the inside sleeve and the collage of items including the album sleeve to *Sounds Like Ska*; a 7" single by The Creation; a photo of Tower Bridge, among other London landmarks; a 100 Club matchbook (used); photos of the band in their original black suits and a pair of dice showing double six (which might refer to the 'Double Six' guitar made in the 1960s by the Burns guitar company, or it might not). And when you took the record out of its sleeve, the centre label was a target, beloved of mods and the RAF, respectively.

The sleeve itself is a sparse affair, Weller and Buckler (with cigarette) sat and Foxton stood in an empty room. Where are the mod cons? Maybe the sleeve is telling us that these three are the mod cons, and what else could you possibly need to make your life easier and more enjoyable in these modern yet uncertain times?

Unlike *In The City*, which was the live set put to record, and *Modern World*, which was an incoherent mish-mash of half-thought-through ideas, *All Mod Cons* was the complete studio album. This is not to say all the songs were complete when Weller introduced them to Foxton and Buckler, some were very much band efforts. Weller:

> Some songs I would come in with a very definite idea of the arrangement and would play it on an acoustic or electric guitar and say this is the verse, chorus, bridge … other times, it was the bare bones of an idea that we would cook up in the studio or rehearsal room or whatever.

The arrangements are more complex and there's a huge leap forward in songwriting and musicianship. A decision was made on the production side and Chris Parry was ousted. (A quick look at the various record covers of this period shows that it was something of a messy departure. However, as on the 'David Watts'/'A'-Bomb' single, the production is credited to Vic Smith and Chris Parry, but 'Tube Station' is Vic Coppersmith-Heaven, though Parry is credited as 'associate producer' on four of the tracks on *All Mod Cons* and The Jam are credited with the arrangements. Are you still with me?)

Vic Coppersmith-Heaven (now using his full surname rather than the more prosaic 'Smith') introduced simple studio techniques such as tracking and overdubs to fill out the basic three-piece. To my thinking, there is also a line that can be traced through many of the songs making it as much of a concept album, or as little of a concept album depending on your point-of-view, as the following year's *Setting Sons* is always talked about being. But this album almost didn't exist.

With Weller distracted by love and Foxton chastened by the criticism of his *Modern World* efforts, the material they were producing wasn't up to scratch. The demos from early '78 weren't good enough and Polydor were unsure about the future of the band, would there even be a future? Weller said he'd dried up: 'I contributed maybe one or two songs that were pretty fucking awful'. Chris Parry, with his A&R hat on, told them in no uncertain terms they had to sort themselves out. So, Weller temporarily left London, returned home to Woking and began listening to his Kinks records ('From that time onwards I took myself more seriously as a songwriter.')

RAK studios had only been open a couple of years and was state-of-the-art for the times and although there isn't the kind of studio trickery that found itself onto later Jam records, Coppersmith-Heaven brought a more solid sound to *All Mod Cons* and pushed the vocals, so important to The Jam, to the fore.

Despite the record's troubled conception, fans and critics were overwhelmed. Charles Shaar Murray in the *NME* wrote:

One of the handful of truly essential rock albums of the last few years... it'll be the album that makes The Jam real contenders for the crown.

Philip Hall in the *Record Mirror* is no less effusive:

This is Sixties music handled in an original and modern way, which has given The Jam their distinctive and now truly distinguished style... one of the three albums of '78.

Melody Maker's Frances Lass, however, put a different spin on it:

Perhaps if Paul Weller were to be a little less enthusiastic, a little less concerned with churning out singles like a bottle factory, The Jam would not be in danger of becoming tiresome.

Of course, everyone is entitled to their own opinion, but that doesn't mean their opinion isn't entirely wrong. Ignoring the critics for a moment, and really, who gives two fucks about their reviews, on the *NME* readers' end-of-year poll, *All Mod Cons* was named the best album of 1978 and what the fans said was always more important to The Jam. It also saw a fundamental shift in The Jam's perspective. Weller: 'It was from that point we got our sound together and our focus and, more importantly, we got an audience'.

'All Mod Cons' (Weller)

Where 'Art School' was introduced with a raucous '1-2-3-4', 'All Mod Cons' has a more measured '1-2-3-4', and it's the same with the guitar; power chords played staccato but in a more controlled way. And it's clear within the first few seconds that *All Mod Cons* is a very different beast from that which had gone before. Sung in the first person, it's an unsubtle attack on the very people Weller had left behind in London as he decamped to Woking to get over the criticism of *Modern World*:

> Seen you before,
> I know your sort,
> You think the world awaits your every breath.

As the opening lines to both the song and the album, Weller sets out his stall from the off and doesn't let up.

> But when we're skint,
> Oh God forbid,
> You drop us like hot bricks.

(Often replaced by 'hot shit' live, in keeping with Weller's penchant for a well-placed expletive). There must have been the fear in the back of his mind that this would, in fact, be the last Jam album, so why not go out all guns blazing?

A thundering solo bass line mid-song, followed by a searing guitar lick, there's not a lyric wasted to bury the record company execs and hangers-on. Everything you need to know about the record industry in one minute and 19 seconds.

'To Be Someone (Didn't We Have A Nice Time)' (Weller)

When 'All Mod Cons' and 'To Be Someone' were played in the same live set, they would usually segue into one another, the lyrical content being in roughly the same ballpark. But whereas 'All Mod Cons' was from the point of view of the pained artist who'd experienced the wrong side of perceived artistic failure, 'To Be Someone' is the fantasy of someone who can only dream of what success brings, any kind of success.

To be someone must be a wonderful thing,
A famous footballer or rock singer,
Or a big film star,
Yes, I think I would like that.

The song goes on to list the things a young man would want; the money, the drugs, the girls; 'to be number one, and liked by everyone'. In the hands of most writers, this would be the theme for the whole song, and it might even have a happy ending, as it were. The music reflects the dreamlike thoughts of the boy, ringing guitars and melodic bass, everything's going to be OK in his dream world.

However, by now, Weller had become a more cynical creature and, at the flick of a switch, the mood changes. The guitars are more strident, the bass pulsates (briefly in the 'Taxman' rhythm that everyone pointed out when 'Start!' was released but, to my knowledge, was never mentioned at the time of 'To Be Someone'.) The list of wonderful things is still intact, but now with menacing accusations and 'no more drinking when the club shuts down'.

There's no more swimming in a guitar-shaped pool,
No more reporters at my beck and call,
No more cocaine, now it's only ground chalk,
No more taxis, now we'll have to walk.

Then our boy shouts to no one because no one is listening, 'Didn't we have a nice time'. There's no question mark because it's not a question, it's a scream of anger and pain. The menace and vitriol with which Weller spits this line out, supposedly, remember, from a character who has yet to experience the finer things that fame offers, firmly puts Weller in the boy's shoes; you might not have experienced this stuff, but I have, and I can see it ebbing away.

The song then changes again, back to the dream, 'I realise I should have stuck to my guns', before skewing back to the angry young man for one last round of 'Didn't we have a nice time' before ending, again, in wistful mode, 'To be someone must be a wonderful thing'.

It's schizophrenic in its approach and perhaps points to Weller's situation at the time; after years of being in the band, doing everything in his power to make the dream of getting signed and making records happen, the reality when things start to go wrong is hard to take.

'To Be Someone' is the best vocal performance that Weller had put on vinyl to date, and as the album unfolds, the listener realises that what's being laid before them is the band laying waste to the three-chord new wave of *In The City* and, in *All Mod Cons*' cohesion, leaves *Modern World* in the cold. The Jam were beginning to find their sound.

'Mr. Clean' (Weller)

Now firmly ensconced in the Ray Davies school of songwriting, Weller creates a character that could be any kind of civil servant, bank manager, or, looking at the lyrics to 'All Mod Cons' and 'To Be Someone', you'd be forgiven for thinking it was again about the music industry. The song starts with a plaintive three-chord riff, underscored by a throbbing bass line, and continues with a third-person diary entry of the eponymous star of the song. So far, so obvious. But it's not long before Weller changes tack and becomes directly threatening:

> If you see me in the street look away,
> 'Cos I don't want to ever catch you looking at me, Mr. Clean.
> 'Cos I hate you, and your wife,
> And if I get the chance, I'll fuck up your life'.

The empathy shown to the la-la-la-la-la-la-la London Girl on *Modern World* is striking by its absence and there is only scorn, sarcasm and derision for this faceless bureaucrat and his unfulfilled dreams and ambitions as Weller does one of his favourite lyrical tropes and simply makes a list:

> Getting pissed at the annual office do,
> A smart blue suit and you went to Cambridge too.
> You miss Page Three but The Times is right for you,
> And Mum and Dad are very proud of you.

Leaving aside the lyrical and musical dexterity of the song, which shows The Jam to be gifted musicians and Weller as a lyricist with great scope and depth, the sentiment behind the track might gall a little as this everyman is attacked by a musician barely out of his teens and who had never really done what most dads would call 'a proper day's work' in his life. Still hasn't, for that matter.

'David Watts' (Davies)

7" double A-side (with "A' Bomb in Wardour Street') cat. no. 2059 054
Recorded at Polydor Studios, London
Produced by Vic Coppersmith-Heaven and Chris Parry
UK release date: 11 August 1978
Highest UK chart placing: 25

That Weller had taken to Ray Davies so deeply is displayed with this relatively little-known Kinks track. The original is a typical Davies vocal performance; light and wistful as he narrates his desire to be like the titular hero. The Jam, who by now had put half a dozen covers onto vinyl, do what The Jam do and smash it to bits. The main vocal was taken by Foxton, 'I can't remember why', whilst Weller takes the bridge, and with its 'fa-fa-fa-fa-fa-fa-

fa-fa' intro, it thunders along at quite a lick while not adding anything to the original other than pace. But coming from the pen of Ray Davies, the lyrics take us on the protagonist's flight of fancy:

And when I lie on my pillow at night,
I dream I could fight like David Watts.
Lead the school team to victory,
And take my exams and pass the lot.

Despite being well received critically, with Garry Bushell writing in *Sounds* that the song was 'a sign that the widespread and blasé criticism of the band as a spent force was a trifle premature', the single only reached number 25, but it showed The Jam still had muscle and, backed as it was with ''A'-Bomb', could still outplay, outwrite and outthink, any of the old punk bands who were sounding more and more dated and who would either implode or decamp to America to take the Yankee dollar.

'English Rose' (Weller)

Not credited on the album song listing, 'English Rose' is a very simple tune of a young man a long way from home and missing his girlfriend (Weller wrote the song whilst the band were touring the US with Blue Öyster Cult and being booed off stage every night). Played on acoustic guitar, its simple circular chord sequence backs the plaintive lyric and has a well-timed key change in the second half of the song, which gives the track the lift it needs to stop it from being, in all honesty, a bit boring – though that is the tightrope that a deeply personal song treads. The sound of waves lapping the shore, the call of a ship's foghorn and the echo on the vocal are added to increase the feeling of isolation but are a bit hammy and, frankly, unnecessary.

No matter where I roam,
I will return to my English Rose,
For no bonds,
Can ever keep me from she.

The reason the song wasn't credited, and why the lyrics were missing from the inner sleeve, is open to conjecture: either the song was added to the album too late for them to be included, or Weller simply felt a little embarrassed. It's also been noted that Weller thought, without the music, the words meant little, from which we can assume that he thought the lyrics to the other songs on *All Mod Cons* were able to stand by themselves. I'm more than inclined to agree with him.

If the songs on the album so far showed Weller at his most accusatory, 'English Rose' brought Weller's tender side into the open. It's not easy for someone who had a natural tendency to keep himself to himself. Indeed, as the band's fame grew, the situation Weller found himself in, the hated 'Spokesman For A Generation', would be increasingly at odds with his own personality.

'In The Crowd' (Weller)

'When I'm in the crowd, I don't see anything', says the opening line. A 180° about-face from 'The Combine' and 'when you're in a crowd, you see things as they really are'.

Introduced by hand-picked guitar chords (very similar in style to 'Mr. Clean'), a pitter-patter bassline and rat-a-tat cymbals, the song begins in a very light mood musically but soon falls into a jumpy rhythm accentuated by Foxton, and Buckler's crashing drums. Listening to the album now, the band seem to grow in maturity and skill with each tune. The song itself continues with Weller's Orwellian vision of society led by unknown faces that tell us what we want and what we need, and encourage us to buy the latest faddy things, 'technology is the most', and where this stealing of our own will is taking place: 'I fall into a trance at the supermarket'.

Younger readers might want to substitute 'supermarket' for 'the internet', but the sentiment, and, for that matter, the outcome, is much the same. The supermarket is a metaphor for society; unthinking and unquestioning.

> And everyone seems that they're acting a dream,
> Cause they're just not thinking about each other,
> And they're taking orders, which are media-spawned,
> And they should know better, now you have been warned.

The song carries on in the same vein, but then, almost exactly halfway through, there's a dramatic change as the tune shifts rhythm and becomes a cauldron of off-beat drums, backwards guitars and an echoed refrain borrowed from *In The City's* 'Away From The Numbers'. If, to date, the band's basic idea was to record their songs as they'd be played live, 'In The Crowd' turns that idea on its head and, at times, is reminiscent of The Beatles' 'Tomorrow Never Knows' from their 1966 album *Revolver*. Weller noted in *The Making of All Mod Cons* that producer Vic Coppersmith-Heaven had introduced the idea of overdubbed guitars and general studio trickery and 'In The Crowd' takes that to its logical conclusion and throws the kitchen sink at it, adding piano as the song, and side one of the album, fades out. Unusually for a Jam recording at this point, Foxton's bass is almost out of the mix, but very much to the front, and adding to the general cacophony, is Buckler's most ambitious drumming to date and it's difficult to believe that it was done in one take. Buckler:

> The drum track went down first, and I would always do the whole thing in one take. That's not to say I didn't have several goes at it, but... we never dropped bits in or borrowed from other takes.

And if Buckler was pushing himself to become better, Weller and Foxton duetting through much of the song, adding muscle to the melody, emphasised that 'the rhythm section' was an integral part of the band, if it ever needed emphasising.

The song remained in The Jam's set for the rest of their career and was the opening track when they performed live on TV for the last time on the debut of music show *The Tube*, introduced by a very young Jools Holland. In this, and later live versions, when the band had added a brass section to the line-up, Weller's overdubbed guitar licks are replicated by the horns, but somehow, rather than add weight to the tune, the short stabs are piercing to the ear and in this case, as in many others, less would have been more.

'Billy Hunt' (Weller)

Initially mooted as the band's fifth single, it was even introduced as such by Weller at a BBC *In Concert* recording on 1 June 1978, 'Billy Hunt' had been written the previous year. The antithesis of David Watts, Billy Hunt (and here we should mention the euphemistic nature of the name, more accurately Silly C**t, as Rick Buckler said, 'I think everyone knows a Billy Hunt') is the kid who has no chance of making anything of his life and so retreats into a fantasy life of James Bond, strippers, Clark Kent and Steve Austin. [Steve Austin was TV's *Six Million Dollar Man*, played by Lee Majors, a US astronaut who suffered a near fatal crash and who was rebuilt with 'bionic' body replacements. An easily understandable reference at the time but another example of how using very contemporary images might become confusing years later.] There's an obvious, and often noted, parallel with Keith Waterhouse's 1959 novel *Billy Liar*. Perhaps the best description of Billy Hunt comes from the jacket of *Billy Liar*; 'The dimmer his surroundings, the more fantastic are his compensatory day-dreams'. Says it all, really.

The song itself is a pretty standard, three-minute Jam track, a great rush of a guitar riff, tight drumming and a rampaging bassline. Although the lyrics clearly show Weller isn't a fan of Billy, they are not without humour and a little sadness, as Weller sings:

No one pushes Billy Hunt around,
Well, they do, but not for long,
When I get fit and grow bionic arms,
The whole world's gonna wish it weren't born.

If these lines are a dark promise of what Billy's thinking, Weller soon shows the more blustery, comic side of Billy.

I could be a superman,
Satisfy any whim that I wanted to,

I could be a human machine,
I could show Steve Austin a thing or two.

The chorus is less of a chorus and more of a taunt as Weller and Foxton sneer 'Billy, Billy Hunt' as many times as they can before the song ends. Poor old Billy Hunt.

'It's Too Bad' (Weller)
Coming in on Weller's chunky guitar sequence and disco sixteenths played by Buckler on the hi-hat, 'It's Too Bad' is a straight pop song. There's no aggression in the lyrics, no snarling, no feedback or scraping the plectrum down the E string, it's simply a tune about lost love and perhaps about his old friend Steve Brookes.

It's too bad that we had to break up,
And too much said for us to ever make up,
I could get by if I could just forget you,
But things remind me and I feel so sad now.

Perhaps the Brookes link is pushing it too far as Weller refers to 'girl' throughout the lyric, but it's a thought worth having for a second or two. More likely is the fact he'd moved out of the flat he shared with his girlfriend in London and back to his parents in Woking to rediscover his songwriting. What 'It's Too Bad' shows is Weller's ease at writing a love song, a marked development from the debut album's 'I've Changed My Address'. Whatever the reality, Weller's vocal is tender and longing – there's even an attempt at falsetto at one point – and the whole thing rides along with an easy grace as he bemoans what has slipped through his fingers:

I could say I'm sorry,
But it's not the point is it?
You want to play your games and,
You don't mind if I get hurt.

The vocal interplay of Weller and Foxton, which had been clear since *In The City*, became even more a part of the band's sound as they developed and is showcased on the repeated refrain at the end of the song.

'Fly' (Weller)
If 'It's Too Bad' is a fairly standard Jam song, 'Fly' is anything but. It is an excellent example of how the band were writing songs with many different parts, not always connecting in a smooth way but always interesting and pushing themselves to create songs outside any generic formula that most bands inevitably fall into, The Jam included.

Opening with acoustic guitar and Weller vocal, most people will have expected another 'English Rose':

The way that sunlight flits across your skirt,
Makes me feel I'm from another world,
To touch your face in the morning light,
I hope you're always gonna be around.

The delivery is almost spoken, wilting and wishful, but then Foxton's bass enters, following the acoustic part note for note, before Buckler raises the tune to a different level. The longing is clear in the vocal delivery, and the lyrics are arguably Weller's most poetic to date, and certainly more engaging than 'English Rose', which was far too personal for the lyrics to truly hit home.

The times I struggle to understand why,
The ancient proverbs like who am I?
Why am I here and what have I done?
I see the answers place my trust in you

The middle eight arrives laden with oohs and aahs, and the back and forth between verse, chorus and bridge keeps the listener guessing as to what might come next. In the end, though, it's all about love, plain and simple.

Love is all sorrow,
Still I'll meet you tomorrow,
I'll look forward to see you,
Now I can't live without you.

'The Place I Love' (Weller)
Opening with a slick two-chord riff and continuing with a choppy rhythm copied by the bass and drums, 'The Place I Love' is lyrically related to 'All Mod Cons' and 'To Be Someone' and tells of the writer's distrust and alienation of London.

The place I love is nowhere near here,
Not within a yard of those trendy dos.
Where dogsbodies pick you up, and graciously give you a lift,
With cherished thoughts and bitterness.

Here he dreams of being in the pastoral setting of 'beautiful moss and colourful flowers', about as far away as you can get from the grimy streets of London, which he'd adored and longed to be a part of for most of his teenage years, and where the juxtaposition of town and country is neatly encapsulated in one line, a place 'with neon lighting controlled by lightning'.

The idea of the countryside being a place of comfort and safety and a past heavy with nostalgia would appear in tracks over the coming years but, for now, Weller sees it as a place where a line can be drawn.

I'm making a stand against the world,
There's those who would hurt us if they heard.

It's a slight song in the context of much of the album's harsh lyrical content, but a song where naivety conquers all is a comforting two minutes before we're dragged back to harsh realities.

As I said in my introduction, I think the order in which songs appear on an album is important, and I think that artists, certainly in pre-digital times, thought the same. That 'The Place I Love' appears where it does, directly before two of the most excoriating tracks that Weller had penned to date, and that's something considering the subjects of *All Mod Cons*, is Weller luring the listener into a false sense of security. Maybe the world's not such a bad place after all. Well, you'd be wrong.

"A' Bomb In Wardour Street' (Weller)
7" double A-side (with 'David Watts') cat. no. 2059 054
Recorded at Eden Studios, London
Produced by Vic Coppersmith-Heaven and Chris Parry
UK release date: 11 August 1978
Highest UK chart placing: 25
Although 'David Watts' amassed most airplay from the double A-side single, it was 'A-Bomb' that said more about The Jam as a band. It's also a brilliant example of Weller's ability to put across the gist of a song in the opening lines:

Where the streets are paved with blood,
With cataclysmic overtones,
Fear and hate linger in the air,
A strictly no-go deadly zone.

After the longing vocal delivery of 'The Place I Love', 'A-Bomb' drops us right back into the screaming, angry Weller, but it's aggression not aimed at advocating violence – that was never part of The Jam's make-up – but to wake people up to what's happening in the country 'in the shape of a size ten boot'. As Weller says, 'It seems like madness to me'.

The idea for the song came from an experience Weller had in London's Vortex club (named in the song), 'It was very heavy, and everyone was only there for the violence, and kicking each other in'. Weller asks of himself:

I don't know what I'm doing here,
'Cos it's not my scene at all.

Buckler starts the song with a cowbell accentuated across the snare and bass drum before a staccato guitar and bass join. There is no running bassline from Foxton this time; he simply matches Weller chord for chord, the sparseness of the music giving space for Weller's lyrics to hit home. The band performed the song on the BBC's *Old Grey Whistle Test*, and although they were moving away from the suits and Union Jack look, they somehow succumbed for this TV show. Dressed in black jackets and white trousers, with Weller's amp draped in a Union flag, it's a blistering, intense performance and brilliantly demonstrates Weller's ability to play lead and rhythm at the same time. Stepping awkwardly in a straight line between amp and mic, chopping away at his Rickenbacker, the moves are straight from the Wilko Johnson playbook. At the end of the song, as Weller describes Britain in a neat, concise way,

A Philistine nation,
Of degradation,
Of hate and war.

He points accusingly ahead of him before literally spelling out what is in store for us,

It's Doctor Martin's,
A.P.O.C.A.L.Y.P.S.E.
Apocalypse!

It's little wonder the BBC chose 'David Watts' for its playlist.

'Down In The Tube Station At Midnight' (Weller)
7" cat. no. POSP 8
Record at RAK Studios, London
Produced by Vic Coppersmith-Heaven
UK release date: 6 October 1978
Highest UK chart position: 15

The band's sixth single almost never made it as Weller said years later, 'I almost bottled out of doing it'. Indeed, producer Vic Coppersmith-Heaven recalled that Weller had thrown the completed lyrics 'in the bin' and it was only after he'd rescued them and convinced Weller there was something to work on that the song was taken seriously. By the end of the recording, Coppersmith-Heaven was down in St. John's Wood tube station with a portable recorder recording trains entering and leaving.

The third track released from the album – the most songs The Jam ever released from a single LP – 'Tube Station' was an astonishing record lyrically and musically and showed the band as being far more inventive than might have been guessed from the first two albums. 'Tube Station' takes the character-driven storytelling of Ray Davies, so bright and optimistic in the heady days of 1960s London, and transports it forward a decade, unceremoniously dumping it in the dangerous, grubby streets of the late 1970s capital. The song is so lyrically complete, and so clear in its message, that it's a three-minute play in itself and would have been a good basis for a BBC *Play For Today* if anyone had had the good sense to have had it made. It would have been interesting to see what the band might have made of the video but, astonishingly, given the value of videos today, there is no official promo of the single. (Though perhaps with the quality of the band's video output to date, we've been spared rather than denied.)

The scene is set with the opening rumble of a tube train and chattering voices, noises that may have been every day for Londoners, but for a 13-year-old in Sheffield, it had a sense of foreboding, tension and worry; you knew it wasn't going to end well. Pushed along by Foxton's spidery bassline and Buckler's insistent hi-hat sixteenths, Weller's guitar, for the first time, takes a back seat, only adding harsh chops at the end of each verse's opening couplets. The story tells of a man on his way home from work, take-away in hand and of his wife waiting at home. Things then take a turn for the very worse:

I first felt a fist, and then a kick,
I could now smell their breath.
They smelt of pubs, and Wormwood Scrubs,
And too many right-wing meetings.

The lyrics are wholly uncompromising, and you have to wonder at the lyricist who would write 'my head's been kicked in and blood's started to pour' and expect it to get played on daytime Radio One. Throughout the song, Weller displays empathy for the man – completely missing in 'Mr. Clean', despite both characters being part of the same commuter drudgery – and ends with the horrific:

I glanced back at my life,
And thought about my wife,
'Cos they've took the keys,
And she'll think it's me.

The imagery in the lyrics is the starkest Weller had produced so far, even considering ''A'-Bomb' and, although I've chosen some to illustrate the story, in picking out certain lines over others, it does a disservice to those which I haven't chosen, and 'Tube Station' needs to be read as a whole. There's not a single word wasted. 'Tube Station' is the song where The Jam got everything right.

The single – the cover is a photo of the band. Guess where? – made it to number 15 in the charts, not as high as 'All Around The World', but it was so far ahead in terms of songwriting; it showed the band making huge strides, and they never looked back. Even the naysayers couldn't deny the power and mastery of the song and it made fans and critics alike eager to hear what the album had to offer as 'Tube Station' was released a full month before the album. And, as we've seen, *All Mod Cons* properly introduced The Jam as the band to watch and the band to beat. In fact, for the next four years, no one got near to reaching them as Weller's quest to be 'bigger than The Beatles' began to gather momentum.

'So Sad About Us' (Townshend)
B-side to 'Down In The Tube Station At Midnight'
Keith Moon, The Who's flamboyant, brilliant drummer, died on 7 September 1978. The Jam happened to be in the studio at the time and it was an easy decision to record a tribute to one of the band's great influences. The song had been in The Jam's live set for a while and took little rehearsing, and the recording itself is a fairly straight copy of The Who's original. The decision was made to release it as the B-side to the soon-to-be-released 'Down In The Tube Station At Midnight'. A black and white portrait of Moon looking his 1965 best eyes us from the back of the single's cover.

'The Night' (Foxton)
B-side to 'Down In The Tube Station At Midnight'
Originally due to be the only song on the B-side of 'Tube Station', another Foxton track, 'The Night', is a short, sharp story of high jinks in a seaside town. The music is very new wave, choppy and insistent and opens with a sleazy harmonica riff. Between the lines of the verses, there's a sort of slide guitar, not in the country sense, more of a chord dragged up the neck, but it adds some interest to the two-chord arrangement, and Weller adds a slick R&B lick between the lines of the bridge.

The lyrics are simplistic; after all, it's just a night out:

Go to the pub, dance for a while,
Have a drink or so.
Please ourselves, do what we want,
Tonight's ours to have fun.

'The Night' is something of an anomaly in that, other than a chorused shout of the title, there are no backing vocals. This time, Foxton does the decent thing and keeps it to a very brief one minute 48 seconds as the song cuts itself off in a very abrupt manner.

Although the tune was written around the time of the *All Mod Cons* sessions, it would have been better placed on the *Modern World* album, and would have enhanced that album with its sharp brevity, but it's nowhere near the quality that Weller produced for the band's game-changing third long player.

'Strange Town' (Weller)

7" cat. no. POSP 34
Recorded at RAK Studios, London
Produced by Vic Coppersmith-Heaven
UK release date: 9 March 1979
Highest UK chart placing: 15

By now, The Jam were really getting into their stride, and what a stride it was. Opening with the urgency of a band who knew where they were going and wanted to get there as quickly as possible, the rampaging bassline and the double-timed snare beats career along at pace as Weller's guitar chops, rather than breaking up the rhythm, propel the song forward. Musically, 'Strange Town' is as dynamic as anything the band had done to date, and Weller's blistering solo, complete with the customary top E string plectrum scratch, perfectly matches the insistent energy. And then, after the third verse repeats the first and you think the song will fade out, it completely changes tack, with a falsetto 'strange town' and then the repeated invitation to 'break it up, break it'.

The strange town of the title is London (the video makes it clear, but more of that later) and follows Weller's obvious changing views of the capital and, by extension, the music business that he lambasted on *All Mod Cons*. What happened to the teenager who was smitten by London, who would spend weekends going to gigs, taking in the punk scene and showing a keen longing to be part of it? After less than two years since the release of *In The City*, the pressure, the criticisms and setbacks, and the physically draining touring, TV and radio shows, Weller was a stranger in what he'd come to view as his city.

Lyrically, it tells of the obvious issues of anyone who found themselves in a strange town, relying on the A-Z (no Google maps back then), everyone ignoring you (London) and 'being betrayed by your accent and manners'. But perhaps the most telling lyric comes in the middle eight:

I've finished with clubs where the music's loud,
'Cause I don't see a face in a single crowd,
There's no one there.

Once again, Weller conjures up the image of the crowd, and the idea introduced in *All Mod Cons*'s 'In The Crowd', that of loneliness and alienation despite the mob that surrounds you and punches the message through.

I look in the mirror, but I can't be seen,
Just a thin, clean layer of Mr. Sheen,
Looking back at me.

Although video promos were still in their relative infancy in 1979, The Jam's on/off use of the medium meant that most of their efforts so far had been performance pieces to the camera. 'Strange Town' broke the mould for all of 14 seconds. The song opens with the band in the London underground, Weller with A-Z in hand, as they attempt to look lost. One can only assume that whatever was in the mind of the director it was abandoned, and the next cut is to Weller's 'Jam shoe' tapping the rhythm, and what follows is fairly run-of-the-mill as far as a video is concerned. The band seem to be filming in an actual venue, making one assume it was shot during a soundcheck, with a small, white neon 'The Jam' sign flashing like the clappers behind them. This is what passed as a light show in 1979, but then The Jam were never about showy gimmicks; the music was all that was needed.

Although the single stalled at number 15 on the chart, the same as 'Tube Station', where 'Tube Station' was on the chart for seven weeks, 'Strange Town' hung around for 13. It gave them another outing on *Top Of The Pops* – indeed, every 7" release garnered them a *Top Of The Pops* performance – with the band dapperly kitted out in boating blazers, Weller in shades and with him and Foxton playing matching Rickenbackers, blonde with a white scratchplate. For the final verse, Weller and Foxton share a mic in a sort of Harrison/McCartney pastiche/homage.

'The Butterfly Collector' (Weller)
B-side to 'Strange Town'
It's often been noted The Jam gave value for money in terms of singles. Only a few appeared on albums, and some of their best songs never appeared on an album at all, at least until the *Best of...* compilations began to appear after the group's demise, and B-sides were no exception. 'The Butterfly Collector' is the first great B-side, opening with a downbeat, heavily reverbed, three-note, picked guitar riff. It's clear from the lyrics that the song is about a 'certain type' of woman – the woman in question here apparently being one 'Catwoman', a notorious figure at punk and new wave gigs at the time.

And the small fame that you've acquired,
Has brought you into cult status,
But to me you're still a collector.

The doleful delivery of the verses suggests there is no mockery, only sadness – 'I don't care about morals' – before the up-tempo chorus becomes far more accusatory:

There's tarts and whores but you're much more,
You're a different kind 'cos you want their minds,
And you just don't care 'cos you've got no pride,
It's just the face on your pillowcase,
That thrills you.

63

It's interesting to note two things about the single's artwork. It's the first time that a picture of the band wasn't used, suggesting that they felt secure enough in themselves that a clearly identifiable band shot wasn't necessary. And as they had spent the 18 months since being signed on the front of just about every music paper and magazine available at the time, and, as noted, every single garnering a *Top Of The Pops* appearance, amongst many other TV shows, it's an understandable assumption. Secondly, the poem on the reverse of the sleeve (over a picture of a butterfly, more striking Jam literalness), uncredited but written by Weller, points to the singer having literary ambitions. The poem is a sarcastic dig at fame:

GREET YOUR NEW MESSIAH,
HE COMES IN FIVE DIFFERENT FLAVOURS.

And at the end, Weller admits that honesty is not a commodity that the world has a lot of:

Of course, secretly I'm in love with the world
And, secretly I think it loves me.
But like all lovers we have tiffs
And it walks off and sulks.
And the sky turns black
With a hundred lies.
Told to and by ourselves.

Later the same year, Weller set up Riot Stories, a publishing imprint that was intended to give young poets a chance to be read, Dave Waller being one of the first to benefit with his book *Notes From Hostile Street*. Another Riot Stories publication was *Mixed Up, Shook Up,* which again was intended to showcase the talent of young poets. One of those poets, Paul Drew, had written a poem titled *Entertainment*, a stream-of-consciousness attack on the hollowness of modern living, which ended with the line, 'it's all the same, that's entertainment'. I'll leave you to think about that. In 1980, Weller set up his own fanzine *December Child*, though it only lasted three issues, where he published his own poetry alongside that of other contributors.

'When You're Young' (Weller)
7" cat. no. POSP 69
Recorded at Eden Studios, London
Produced by Vic Coppersmith-Heaven
UK release date 17 August 1979
Highest UK chart placing: 17
'Life is timeless, days are long when you're young'. The opening line, which closely follows confident shouts of 'woa-o-ho', leads us to believe that Weller

Above: From the 'News Of The World' photo shoot. Foxton appears to have sobered up. (*Alamy*)

Left: *In The City*: 'There's a thousand things I wanna say to you'. Over the next five years, Weller would spell most of them out. (*Polydor*)

Below: All wrapped up with somewhere to go. An early publicity shot.

Right: Polydor wring every last bit of cash out of the band with this reissue for the 'In The City' single in 2002. Expect 50th anniversary releases coming to an internet outlet near you in 2027.

Above: From the 'In The City' video, Weller is doing his scratch-along-the-E-string thing.

Right: Call that a light show? A full band shot from the 'Strange Town' video.

Left: Generally regarded as not good enough, *This Is The Modern World* could have been the end for the band. (*Polydor*)

Right: *NME* cover stars way back in '78.

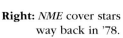

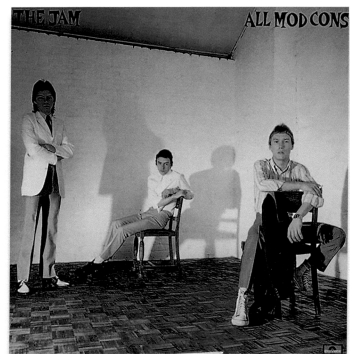

Right: The album
that marked The
Jam as contenders,
All Mod Cons kick-
started their rise to
the top. (*Polydor*)

Left: The 'Down In
The Tube Station
At Midnight' single.
Nothing if not
literal. History does
not record if it was
actually midnight.
(*Polydor*)

Left: *Setting Sons*: though the three figures weren't meant to be read as the band, I like to think it's Foxton and Buckler aiding Weller, the central figure. I do love a good metaphor. (*Polydor*)

Right: 'Those braying sheep on my TV screen'. The rear cover of the European release of 'Going Underground' with the author's own Tootal scarf. Every Mod's must-have item of clothing.

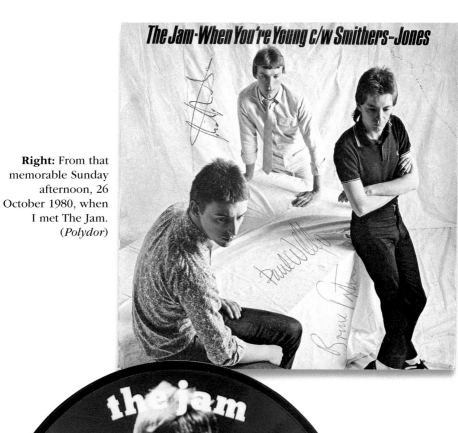

Right: From that memorable Sunday afternoon, 26 October 1980, when I met The Jam. (*Polydor*)

Left: 7" picture disc of an interview with Weller after a show promoting *Setting Sons*. Weller said they had nothing to do with the mod revival, 'maybe a pair of shoes or a tie'.

Left: A pastiche album sleeve, but the music was entirely their own. No cover versions on *Sound Affects*. (*Polydor*)

Right: Music paper *Melody Maker* arranged a meeting between Weller and Pete Townshend in 1980. It didn't go well. (I wonder what happened to the band on the hand-written poster?). (*Jeanette Beckman*)

Right: Front of the 7" import single of 'That's Entertainment' from Germany. It reached number 21 in the UK charts.

Left: Rear of the same single. Note the candy stripe that appeared later in the form of a gift with *The Gift* album.

Right: The music press hits the nail on the head. From the *NME* circa. 1980.

Left: A flexidisc released with *Flexipop* magazine. 'Place coin here if flexible record slips'.

Right: 'Start!' Japanese 7". It's hard to tell what's going on with Foxton's hair. But then again, it always was.

Left: Side one of a 7" US radio sampler. Side two is 'My Generation' by little-known British four-piece The Who.

Right: The Front cover of a US 12" single. The photo shoot was at Chiswick House because The Beatles were there in 1966 for 'Paperback Writer'. Where The Beatles went, The Jam followed.

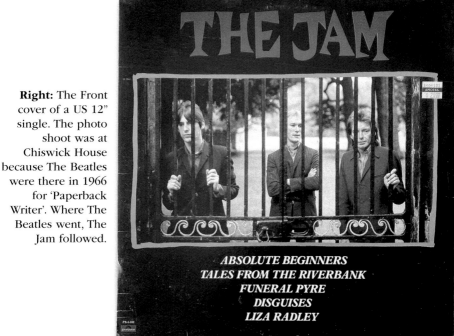

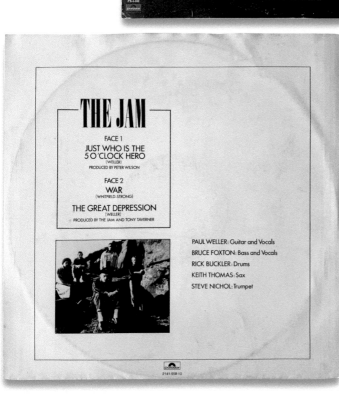

Left: Rear of the 12" version of 'Just Who Is The Five O'Clock Hero?' with The Jam's expanded five-piece and a production credit for Tony Taverner.

Left: Cover of the *Trans Global Express* tour programme, using the album cover of *The Gift*. It's a little creased due to where I had to keep it whilst pogoing in the mosh pit.

Right: A little tattered and torn, but not bad for a forty-year-old. The paper bag that came with the *The Gift* album. (*Polydor*)

Right: Cover of the *A Solid Bond In Your Heart* tour programme. Begging the question, why was it 'Beat Surrender' and not 'Solid Bond' that was the band's last single?

Left: 'Town Called Malice' 7" featuring Rick Buckler's uncredited photo taken from the tour bus. (*Polydor*)

Left: Uncredited caricatures from the *Solid Bond* tour programme. A friend of mine made the Weller image into a t-shirt for me. I was the envy of the ball.

Right: A last show bootleg, *The Badge*, featuring hits, 'Star', 'Beat', 'The Numbers', 'the Crowd' and 'About Town'. 'Copying, public performance and broadcasting prohibited'. Really?

Right: Front cover of the 'Beat Surrender' 12" featuring Gill Price, the English Rose. (*Polydor*)

Left: The reverse of the 'Beat Surrender' 12". The sleeve reminds us of the quality of The Jam's singles, 16 of them over five years. (*Polydor*)

Above: A clumsy attempt at pop art, notable for Weller's rare red Jam shoes. (*Alamy*)

had found something to be optimistic about, one of his favourite topics, youth. The first verse is crammed with positive statements:

Life is a drink, and you get drunk when you're young.

What can't you do when you're young? When all of life is ahead of you and the world is yours and the possibilities seem endless? Well, hold on youngster...

But you find out life isn't like that,
It's so hard to comprehend,
Why you set up your dreams to have them smashed in the end.

What you give with one hand ...

Weller was still only 21 but knew enough to know that disappointments lay ahead and felt it his duty to introduce a note of caution to those who hadn't yet experienced the lows (although there had been plenty of highs along the way). But his championing of youth had hit a chord with thousands across the UK – I had just turned 14 at the time – and for many of us, Weller was the only person who spoke to us, who understood us and would carry the fight for us. Lyrically, he'd never sounded more mature, some of the lines being the best he'd written to date, and the pithiest he'd ever come up with, blending humour and sarcasm, hope and despair.

It's so hard to understand,
Why the world is your oyster but your future's a clam.
It's got you in its grip before you're born,
It's done with the use of a dice and a board,
And let you think you're king but you're really a pawn.

Considering what was to come in November of 1979, the misfiring concept album *Setting Sons*, 'When You're Young' could be seen as something of an introduction, an anthem for doomed youth (with apologies to Wilfred Owen). Musically, the band had hit their stride with what could generically be called The Jam 'sound' – thrashing power chord guitar, pulsating, running bass lines and solid, driving drums but, although the army of fans was growing, and the live shows were among the best that any band could hope to achieve, the single only made it to number seventeen. Even more disappointing given that their contemporaries in the new wave genre, The Police, The Boomtown Rats, Ian Dury and Gary Numan, were all hitting number one, and seven singles and three albums into The Jam's career, they still hadn't broken the Top Ten. As for the recording itself, despite different attempts to get the final mix to everyone's liking, it was proving a tricky task. Coppersmith-Heaven remembered:

We'd spent four to five thousand pounds and we weren't satisfied with either of the versions we'd done, so I was about to try a third different studio because I thought The Jam were in a good situation where they could plan and wait rather than rushing out something that wasn't right.

However, the Polydor powers that be saw things differently and Weller, his father, John, and Coppersmith-Heaven were called in for a meeting where they were basically told that Coppersmith-Heaven didn't know what he was doing, and it was time for a change. Weller junior would have none of it and defended his producer but, by the time the sessions for *Setting Sons* came around, Weller was beginning to think differently.

Unlike The Jam's previous outings in the world of promo films, 'When You're Young' even tried a 'proper' video, out of the studio and into a park, performing on a bandstand, a modern combo hoping to bring salvation to their army of fans. I think it shows something of the growing confidence the band had in themselves as, for the first time on a promo, they're miming without their amps behind them. It's them saying, 'look at us, we know we can play, we know you know we can play, so what's the point in pretending?' Either that, or they didn't have a big enough car to fit the amps in.

To provide the customary lack of subtlety, a number of young teenagers had been rounded up – all late 1970s non-haircuts and flares – to provide the aforementioned 'woa-o-hos' but, despite Foxton gamely taking on the role of choirmaster, most seemed either puzzled or uninterested, though one of them fist-pumps along to at least show willing. Still, among the shouting and the handclaps, the band seemed genuinely happy to be there, laughing, joking and generally having fun around the more serious business of miming to the song.

The tune rolls in and then cuts to staccato mode, Weller chopping the chords from his Rickenbacker, Foxton and Buckler doing what fans had come to expect, pushing the tune along. The drop-down comes and Buckler changes to playing his snare on the third beat of the bar in a reggae style, though it was as near to that particular musical genre as the band ever came. Weller's taut runs switch in the mix from left to right, before freeing themselves into his solo, the guitar lines soaring above the backing exemplifying the freedom that youth promised but is so quickly snatched away. As the song fades out to the repeated strains of:

All over the country, the lights are going out,
In millions of homes and thousands of flats,
Going out, going out, going out...

The camera pans away and reveals two dogs staring dolefully towards you and you feel they understand.

'When You're Young' will always be a reminder of my most intimate Jam moment when, on October 26 1980, in Sheffield's Top Rank, I nervously offered my record's picture sleeve to the band and, in cheap biro, they scribbled their name as they had done thousands of times before and would do thousands of times again, but it only happened once for me.

'Smithers-Jones' (Foxton)

B-side to 'When You're Young'
Recorded at Townhouse Studios, London
Produced by Vic Coppersmith-Heaven
The track where Foxton comes of age as a songwriter. Although the subject of the downtrodden commuter had already been explored by Weller in 'Mr. Clean', Foxton has a bucketload more sympathy for his creation, perhaps because he'd had a job while The Jam were still finding their feet and had to balance work and the band. The song opens with another pulsating Foxton bassline whilst the lyrics reflect the worries of everyone who needs to be at their place of work at a designated time. In 1979, working from home wasn't an option for most people – Smithers-Jones included.

> Here we go again, it's Monday at last,
> He's heading for the Waterloo Line,
> To catch the 8am fast, it's usually dead on time,
> Hope it isn't late, got to be there by nine.

Our hero is clearly liked as he's informed that the boss wants to see him and 'I hope it's the promotion you've been looking for'. Of course, it's nothing of the sort and (spoiler alert!) Smithers-Jones is destined to become another number on the unemployment register. Foxton's turn of phrase, one of the mealy-mouthed ways of avoiding the stark truth of someone being sacked, 'there's no longer a position for you', is perhaps his greatest line.

And that might have been the end of the story, but Weller, with all his biting cynicism, can't leave it at that and offers his own opinion with an unprovoked attack on Smithers-Jones, beginning with the British reaction to bad news, 'put on the kettle and make some tea', reminding us that 'the only one smiling is the suntanned boss', and finally,

> Work and work and work 'til you die,
> 'Cos there's plenty more fish in the sea to fry.

If Smithers-Jones was already feeling depressed, he'd be suicidal by the end.

Some People Might Say My Life Is In A Rut – Setting Sons To Going Underground

Setting Sons

LP cat. no. POLD 5028
Recorded at The Townhouse Studios, London
Produced by Vic Coppersmith-Heaven
UK release date: 16 November 1979
Highest UK chart placing: 4
Guest musicians:
'Merton' Mick Talbot: piano on 'Heatwave'
Rudi: saxophone
The Jam Philharmonic Orchestra: cello, timpani and recorder
Danny, Dean, Mark, Pete and Martin: hurrahs

The Jam's concept album. Or is it? The answer is 'sort of'. Weller had the idea of writing a story based around three friends who grew up together and meet up after a civil war has taken place. The idealist poet, the realist businessman and the moderator attempting to balance their opposing views. That was the plan at least but, as Weller later admitted, eventually he thought, 'I can't be fucked doing this anymore. Let's just make an album'.

However, it was an idea that was the seed of the album's best songs, but there was pressure coming from Polydor to finish the recording in time for the Christmas market and Weller, never the most prolific of writers, was struggling to come up with material, which explains the orchestral version of 'Smithers-Jones' and the band's tried and trusted trick of sticking a cover version on an album. Weller later said how the pressure had motivated him and motivation, for the most part, is probably a good thing, but when it culminates in songs which are thrown together without the time to properly edit and arrange them, something is going to get lost. As Foxton pointed out in the band's autobiography, *A Beat Concerto*,

> We (Foxton and Buckler) were literally learning (each song) one night and recording it the next day, which is pretty fatal to do. Invariably, you're going to listen to it in a few days' time and think, oh, I wish I'd done that, and that would have been better.

It's a testament to the band's musicianship and desire to improve and be the best they can be because even now, when you listen to the album, it's difficult to see how any of the playing could be improved.

In the end, the concept idea proved to be too ambitious. Although some of the songs obviously fit into this narrative, the greater number don't and it gives the album a fragmented feel. The band themselves saw it as their worst album to date, which I feel is nonsense, but we're all allowed our own opinion. Weller said of the album:

> To me, it was a real letdown. It could have been another group. The sound was really horribly professional, on the verge of being slick. I was never particularly pleased with it.

Producer Vic Coppersmith-Heaven's laborious, and expensive, way of working – he'd spent 15 hours mixing 'Tube Station' and two days on 'Strange Town' – was also something the band would eventually tire of.

The reviews for *Setting Sons* followed the by-now familiar pattern of almost universal praise but with the odd naysayer. Pete Silverton writing for *Sounds* was firmly in the latter court:

> (The Jam) have always settled for working within their own limits. There's no sense of ambition ... (an) understanding that if you go so far, and no further, you'll never go wrong... long may Paul Weller have such modest aims.

The *Record Mirror* saw it differently:

> (*Setting Sons*) is a set of tunes of emotional depth and maturity ... let's just say that *Setting Sons* is a far more ambitious and adventurous project in every respect ... the last great album of the Seventies.

And the *NME*'s Tony Stewart was also a fan:

> There isn't one dubious song among the nine originals ... 'Thick As Thieves' is possibly the best song Weller has ever written...

However, I think Tony loses it towards the end of his review when he says of *Setting Sons*:

> Weller carries (it) alone with his stunning vocals ... propulsive guitar and a batch of melodies and arrangements that put many of the songs on *All Mod Cons* into the shade ... more than ever it's a one-man band ... the success of the album (relies on) his talent alone. It's Paul's best album yet; almost his first solo album, too.

Of course, Weller wrote the majority of The Jam's songs, and certainly the best songs, but this last comment is laughable and if I do anything with this book, it's to demonstrate just how much Weller needed Foxton and Buckler to give flesh to the bones of his ideas.

If The Jam's sound was developing, then much the same can be said of the band's artwork. Still led by in-house Polydor art director Bill Smith, the cover featured a close-up shot of a bronze statue from 1919 called *The St. John's Ambulance Bearers* by Benjamin Clemens. The photographer, Andrew Douglas, had presented his picture to Polydor's art department as a stock image with a view to it being used for an album sleeve, but with no particular album in mind. To a youngster like me who'd only ever seen over-life-size statues 'celebrating' the World Wars, I had an image of an imposing piece of art, whereas the statue is only 67cm (27") tall and might just about squeeze into your aeroplane carry-on suitcase. What the viewer also might not realise from the image is that the two characters on the outside are the St. John's men and are carrying the soldier, in the middle, who has lost the ability to walk unaided. Again, it's easy to stray into the questionable realms of metaphor here but if Weller is the central figure, it's his bandmates who are the props. However, Weller has said he had no part in choosing the image for the album cover, so let's reign in our metaphorical tendencies. What every Jam fan did think at the time, however, was the three figures must relate to the three members of The Jam rather than the intended protagonists of Weller's concept.

The image of the statue was embossed in order to, in Smith's words, 'add a little bite', and the embossing carries onto the rear of the sleeve with an illustrated English rose frame around a photo of a British bulldog sitting next to a Union Jack deckchair on a pebble beach. And if you can't see the self-deprecating humour in that you're not looking properly. As the sleeve was designed before the track listing had been established, there is no list of songs, though a sticker was later added to each copy with the final listing, and I pity the poor intern who got that job. My own copy of the album never had the sticker and to this day, I'm not sure whether it's best to have the sticker or not to have the sticker. I'm also a little concerned about the number of years I've let that question bother me.

The inside sleeve carries lyrics to most of the original songs, 'Girl On The Phone' misses out, over an illustration of the same beach, dog and deckchair, only this time with a pier (Brighton pier?) in the background. The reverse is similar in layout to *All Mod Cons* being a collage, but rather than a hedonistic nod to the 1960s, it draws on martial images of Britain's colonial past, World War One (black and white photos and a military jacket) and what looks like a cigarette card depicting a World War Two German V rocket (which is obviously nothing to do with Britain but all Empires are intrinsically wrong simply by dint of what they are and how they come to be).

The effort put into the album packaging gained some kind of recognition when, in 2001, *Q* magazine made it number 87 in their '100 Best Album Covers Of All Time' and it was number two in the *NME*'s 'Best Dressed (Sleeve)'. More importantly for The Jam, the readers of the *NME* voted it the best album of 1979, giving the band the 'best album' accolade for the second year running.

(And while we're talking of the *NME*'s end-of-year poll; Best Group – winner, Best Songwriter – winner, Best Guitarist – winner, Best Bass Player

– winner, Best Drummer – winner, Best Male Singer – 3rd, Most Wonderful
Human Being (Weller) – 7th. It's fair to say amongst a certain slice of the
record-buying public, The Jam had attained quite a level of popularity.)

'Girl On The Phone' (Weller)

Despite all the talk of concept albums, *Setting Sons* begins with a throwaway
three-minute song describing the unnerving experience of being stalked,
which Weller had experienced in London the previous year, and which was
part of the reason he'd gone home to Woking. It's also a couched allusion
to the press, who by now had decided Weller was the 'Spokesman For A
Generation', an unasked for, though not unmerited, title and would print
stories about him, taking little care as to their veracity. As he later said, it was
about how people seemed to know more about him than he did himself.

'Girl On The Phone' opens with, yep, you've guessed it, the ringing of a
telephone before the song goes on to be what might be called a 'typical'
Jam song. Choppy guitars, the bass line rushing about all over the place and
drums stopping the whole thing from falling apart. Lyrically, we come across
a popular Weller motif of writing in lists:

> Girl on the phone keeps a-ringing back,
> She knows all my details, she's got my facts,
> She tells me my height and she knows my weight,
> She knows my age and says she knows fate.

After the song's abrupt ending, we hear a female voice, actually a French
intern working on the recording studio's reception desk, over a dialling tone
asking, 'Hello, are you there?' before the receiver is replaced on the hook.
(For the sake of clarity, younger readers might want to ask an older relative
what a 'dialling tone', 'receiver' and 'hook' are.)

'Thick As Thieves' (Weller)

The first song on the record that had some connection with the original idea
of a concept album. 'Thick As Thieves' picks up the theme of *In The City*'s
'I Got By In Time', of close friendships loosening over the years as people
grow older, and drift apart as differing adult responsibilities erode that initial
childhood bond.

> Thick as thieves us, we'd stick together for all time.
> And we meant it, but it turns out just for a while,
> We stole the friendship that bound us together.

The song has been seen in differing ways through the years; are the three
friends The Jam? Or perhaps Weller, Waller and Brookes? Whatever the
actuality, its dense musical structure clearly aligns it with the other 'concept

songs'. It rumbles in with drums and bass before Weller's guitar, overdubbed and panned hard left and right (clearly audible if you listen to the tune with headphones), almost apologetically introduces itself. The downbeat atmosphere the music imposes carries what is thematically one of the saddest songs Weller ever wrote, containing more regret and remorse than many a love song.

The track is also difficult to pin down as far as arrangement is concerned. Having grown up with the classic songwriting of Motown, Stax, and The Beatles, Weller's songs up to now had followed a very traditional songwriting pattern of easily discernible verse, chorus, middle-eight, usually with a guitar solo of some kind somewhere in the mix. 'Thick As Thieves' strays from the path and, although it has repeating musical motifs and melodies, its structure is more complex. It also pushes along in a cautiously dynamic way until the song nears the end, when the volume is ramped up for a cutting guitar interjection. This leads to a dropdown of simple bass and drums, leaving the claustrophobic three-piece behind to allow clarity for the last verse. Then the song builds to a crescendo, the lyric 'thick as thieves' repeated over and over, the last lines encapsulating the powerlessness of the protagonists to take control of their own lives, before the song comes to a blazing end.

> But something came along that changed our minds (we're no longer as thick as thieves, no)
> I don't know what and I don't know why (we're not as thick as we used to be, no)
> But we seemed to grow up in a flash of time (we're no longer thick as thieves, no)
> While we watched our ideals helplessly unwind (we're not thick as we used to be, no)

'Private Hell' (Weller)

There is a belief among writers that if you want to speak a truth, then speak about subjects you know and understand. But one of Weller's great gifts as a songwriter is to put himself in the shoes of characters he'll have had little contact with throughout his pop-star life. And a middle-aged mum on the verge of a nervous breakdown was not within Weller's experience; he was still only 21 at the time and from a close, loving family, yet, to my reading, his observations ring as true as in any lauded kitchen sink drama.

If 'Thick As Thieves' is claustrophobic and highlights a feeling of loss of control over your life, 'Private Hell' twists the knife deeper. It's the perfect example of Weller's ability to sum up a song in the opening lines, introducing the theme in a succinct and blatant manner, leaving the listener in no doubt as to where the song is headed:

> Closer than close, you see yourself, a mirrored image,
> Of what you wanted to be.

As each day goes by, you can't remember,
What it was you wanted anyway.

The song tells its story in the clearest way possible and in 'Private Hell' the
message, the story, is told in bleak, direct language:

The fingers feel the lines,
They prod the space,
Your ageing face.
The face that once was so beautiful,
Is still there, but unrecognisable.

In the vein of Ray Davies and 'Waterloo Sunset's Terry and Julie, Weller gives
his characters names; the woman's daughter is Emma, Emma's husband is
Terry (a coincidence, surely) and the woman's son is Edward, away at college
and ignoring our desperate housewife's letters. Weller acknowledges the
strength of the woman's character, but is it worth it? To continue in a loveless
world where your own family is too engrossed in their own lives to care
about each other.

Foxton opens the tune with a foreboding rumble of bass, Buckler attacks
his kit and Weller scratches his Rickenbacker, transporting us to an unsettling
world. The intensity of the track never lets up until, near the end, Foxton is
left alone again but replaces the rumble with an alternating note and octave
mimicking the ticking of a clock. Weller's harmonics, stark, piercing and as
desperate as the housewife, reflect the final lines.

Alone at 6 o'clock,
You drop a cup,
You see it smash,
Inside you crack,
You can't go on,
But you sweep it up,
Safe at last inside your private hell.

'Little Boy Soldiers' (Weller)
Back to the 'concept' narrative, and, for my money, one of the finest anti-war
songs ever written. Despite the mostly traditional songwriting style of Weller,
he was never afraid to introduce twists and turns into The Jam's music and
'Little Boy Soldiers' can be divided into five, very clear sections.

The song opens with a solo Weller picking individual notes on his guitar,
lyrics dripping in sarcasm:

It's funny how you never knew what my name was,
Our only contact was a form for the election.

The rhythm section come into part two as Weller's tired vocal, which is not to say bored sounding, tells us our protagonist doesn't want to go to war, but what option is there but to play his government's 'war games'? Now the song switches, and very unsubtle military drum rolls and the sound of exploding bombs transplant our man onto the battlefield:

I'm up on the hills playing little boy soldiers,
Reconnaissance duty at five thirty,
Shoot, shoot, shoot and kill the natives,
You're one of us and we love you for that.

Then the music changes – whether through key change or modulation, I'm not skilled enough to tell – pushing the vocal to be more strident and forceful, and to remind us of the two things required to make us feel safe in our belief that what we are doing is right:

Think of honour, Queen and country,
You're a blessed son of the British Empire,
God's on our side and so is Washington.

(It's a truism today that whenever a UK government, especially a right-wing, populist government, in tandem with a pliant media, needs the country to accept a course of action that isn't entirely commendable or is even downright distasteful, the rhetoric employed always relates back to Empire and the Second World War. I question if there's a country in the world which feels the need to rest on the crutch of lost glories quite like England, and I specifically say England, not the UK, as England alone seems to be so deeply in hock to the past.)

Weller's voice strains through the repeating refrain, 'We're up on the hills playing little boy soldiers' before part three, just Weller and acoustic guitar, singing sotto voce with an eerie, ghost-like whisper echoing the lyrics, telling 'a tale of how goodness prevailed'.

We ruled the world,
We killed and robbed,
The fucking lot,
But we don't feel bad.

And why don't we feel bad?

It was done beneath the flag of democracy.

Now the song thunders into part four, the protagonist hailing his belief in his actions, the absolute right of what he's doing up on those hills, 'Yes, I do'. Into part five, musically the same as part two, but Weller brings his tale to a close with the inevitable ending and a reminder that, amid the patriotic bluster of a military campaign, people might die:

Then they send you home in a pine overcoat,
With a letter to your mum,
Saying find enclosed one son, one medal and a note to say he won.

A man's life and death told in three and a half minutes. The final chord, augmented by a rolling piano that's introduced for the last few bars, if you listen carefully to the very end, drones on for a full 30 seconds (surely a homage to The Beatles' 'A Day In The Life') and, if you want to read something into it, might be seen as a chance for momentary reflection: do you really want to die for another person's lack of restraint?

'Wasteland' (Weller)

After being pummelled both musically and lyrically by the previous three songs, 'Wasteland' comes as something of a relief, although a dictionary definition might point to something other than relief: 'A wasteland is someplace that's empty and desolate, with no sign of life or growth'.

If we accept the conceit of the three friends that *Setting Sons* was originally meant to be, besides the ideological opposites of the businessman and revolutionary, 'Wasteland' is the voice of the third, the conduit that still hopes to keep the friendship alive:

Meet me on the wasteland later this day,
We'll sit and talk and hold hands, maybe.

More and more, Weller was introducing new sounds and instrumentation in The Jam's work and 'Wasteland' opens with the toot-toot-toot of a recorder, not the most rock and roll of instruments, but it gives the track a plaintive, melodic introduction that neatly balances the most poetic lyrics of the album: 'the smouldering embers of yesterday' is a personal favourite. Our narrator is looking back to a simpler time for the friends with unabashed nostalgia:

We'll talk about the old days,
When the wasteland was release when we could play,
And think without feeling guilty.

But, of course, you can never go back, and the world has changed, not for the good. Weller again uses imagery straight out of Orwell's *1984*, 'to be caught smiling is to acknowledge life', and then uses one of his favoured lyrical devices, the list:

And there amongst the shit, the dirty linen,
The holy Coca-Cola tins, the punctured footballs,
The ragged dolls, the rusting bicycles.

(There's a nice double play with 'holy or 'holey'. Listen to the record and you might immediately think of tins of pop thrown onto the rubbish heap, but the lyric sheet makes it clear Weller is talking about the omniscient being that is the Coca-Cola Company.)

The music may be bright and optimistic, but it's the end for the friends, as they watch the rain tumbling and falling 'exactly like our lives'. Side one of *Setting Sons* ends there, and as the end of the story, it would be a suitably downbeat, and very sad end. But we have side two, which opens with another of the 'concept' songs and puts 'Wasteland' out of order as far as the storyline is concerned.

'Burning Sky' (Weller)
If ever a single word could sum up the attitude and character of a person, the opening line of 'Burning Sky' is an exemplary example as the businessman in the *Setting Sons* concept story, begins a letter to his one-time friend:

How are things in your little world?

'Little'. In that one passive-aggressive word, the world of the businessman is laid before us, and the lyric continues, giving us a deeper insight into this dog-eat-dog, no-time-for-idealists world that has been opened with that six-letter word, more insulting than any four-letter word could ever be.

We know it's a letter as the lyrics, once again helpfully laid before us on the inside sleeve, are set out in this way, starting with 'Dear' on a single line and ending with 'faithfully'. There is little rhyming, just block text as our businessman friend tells the recipient the uselessness of old friendships if they don't add to his burgeoning wealth.

Things are really taking off for me,
Business is thriving, and I'm showing a profit,
And in any case it wouldn't be the same,
'Cause we've all grown up, and we've got our lives,
And the values that we had once upon a time,
Seem stupid now, 'cause the rent must be paid,
And some bonds severed, and others made.

We know it's true that old friendships sometimes run their course; people move away, families start and interests change, but it's the shallowness and disinterest that characterises the businessman's letter and his absolute belief that his vision is the correct vision:

It's only us realists who are gonna come through.

These are the words of a man who is sneering at his once close friends, wrapping it up in the language of 'realism' to find excuses for his behaviour, but who has lost interest in the person he was, and the people he knew. In the end, 'Burning Sky' is less a song than a polemic against naivety.

'Smithers-Jones' (Foxton)
As the original B-side of 'The Eton Rifles', 'Smithers-Jones' pounded along in standard Jam fashion. Here, we have a musical backing by 'The Jam Philharmonic Orchestra', an idea suggested by Rick Buckler. I don't know enough about classical music, its arrangement and playing, to give a reasoned critique, but it sounds OK to me. More than anything this, along with the album's closer, The Vandellas' 'Heatwave', points to a lack of material rather than an attempt to push musical boundaries and introduce The Jam's now massive fanbase to the delights, or otherwise, of classical music.

'Saturday's Kids' (Weller)
With a songbook jam-packed with strident guitars, 'Saturday's Kids' begins with perhaps the most strident of them all, with Buckler's cowbell cutting through in the background. In the context, or concept, of the album, it doesn't mesh, but by now, the whole idea of a concept album is firmly out of the window, though the *NME* called the song 'a brilliant piece of reportage'. It's a personal song about Weller's old haunts in Woking and holiday places on the south coast of England and is a general reflection on life in an English town:

Saturday's boys live life with insults,
Drink lots of beer and wait for half-time results.

Or, on the female side:

Saturdays girls work in Tescos and Woolworths,
Wear cheap perfume cause it's all they can afford.

And what can we hope for our futures?

Save up your money for a holiday,
To Selsey Bill or Bracklesham Bay,
Think of the future when we'll settle down,
Marry the girl next door with one on the way.

It's not painting the most exciting picture.

It's remarkable that Polydor chose it as the B-side to the American release of 'Heatwave'. If the A-side was meant to draw the Americans in with a well-loved and easily recognised soul number, the flip – with its references to Tescos, Cortinas, Babycham and Capstan non-filters – would have left them nonplussed. Far out!

'The Eton Rifles' (Weller)

7" cat. no. POSP 83
Recorded at Townhouse Studios, London
Produced by Vic Coppersmith-Heaven and The Jam
UK release date: 26 October 1979
Highest UK chart placing: 3

'The Eton Rifles' comes crashing in with a repeated, naggingly insistent four-note bassline while Buckler rumbles around the toms giving the musical impression of a thunderstorm, complementing Weller's lightning power chords, an electrical discharge barely in time with the rhythm track. And there's no quarter given as Weller introduces another very British lyric, 'Sup up your beer and collect your fags', crammed with sarcasm and unconcealed distaste for the target, which is literally spelt out in the title. 'The Eton Rifles' is a song Weller presented to Foxton and Buckler almost in its entirety and though there are no drums on the demo, the bassline is written on guitar, leaving Foxton little room to introduce his own style. 'The Eton Rifles' is the first time the band get a production credit.

Strangely, the song doesn't have a formal video, but the band played it on consecutive *Top of The Pops* at the beginning of November. This included, in one memorable performance, four lads dressed in *Setting Sons* album cover style army jackets, on the set simply to shout 'hurray' at the appropriate time. Buckler sports a very Eton-like boating blazer and straw boater. Publicity images for the single included a photo of a straw boater next to a revolver pistol. Let's say it again: The Jam were never ones for subtlety.

Perhaps the best version, however, is when the band open Granada TV's *Something Else* programme, the remit of which was helpfully explained in the most charmingly nervous introduction in television history by Leila Waring (she later remembered '(Weller) sulked and tutted, whilst I fumbled through ten re-takes introducing them'); all the while Weller is just behind her shoulder glaring at the camera the way a lion glares at visitors to a zoo:

Hello, this is *Something Else* from Manchester, and for anyone who doesn't know just what they're in for, I'd better explain. This is a show for people from 16 to 20, though anyone else is more than welcome to watch, and it's been dreamed up and put together by a bunch of eight of us, all in that age group and all living in the Manchester area. There's a bit of everything in the show and, of course, there's lots of music. Here's The Jam with 'Eton Rifles'; it's one of the numbers from their new album.

The band then blast through the song, which includes at the end the extended album version, Weller standing in front of his surprisingly small, Peavey amp, eliciting feedback while crashing through Townshend-esque power chords, ripping his plectrum down the bottom E string and doing the 'Morse code' pick-up thing, all of Weller's favourite guitar tropes in one sublime performance, whilst Buckler and Foxton keep the whole thing together with their nailed down rhythm.

The song was written whilst on a very wet caravanning holiday, the weather being so terrible, Weller stayed in and 'knocked out' five songs. He later told *Uncut* magazine:

> I was watching the news on TV and I saw this footage of a Right To Work march going past Eton, where all the kids from the school came outside and started jeering at the marchers.

Lyrically, it's excoriating in its attack on the privilege of the upper class but concedes that, against the strength of the class system and the establishment which works to uphold that system, the rest of us are doomed to be repeatedly put in our place, 'What chance have you got against a tie and a crest?' asks Weller. The song also contains what, for me, is one of Weller's funniest and most sarcastic lyrics of The Jam's career, as he explains the reasons as to why the working class lost a bloody encounter against their foe, but they're not giving up,

> We were no match for their untamed wit,
> But some of the lads said they'd be back next week.

Listen to the single and you can hear Weller's low voice speaking the words under the melody, adding a brooding sense of determination and solidarity; the fight isn't over yet.

The month after its release, The *Eton College Chronicle* published an interview with Weller and asked him what the song was about. Weller replied:

> Basically, it's taking the mickey out of class. It's meant to be humorous... Two classes clashing, with the trendy revolutionary saying, 'come on, sup up your beer, there's a row on up the road', and it's like, 'The revolution will start after I've finished my pint'... It's not a political song in the sense of 10 Downing Street politics but of everyday politics... I think that everyone has a right to a good education and they're just not getting it. It's the same old story... every man is equal, but some are more equal than others. That still exists.

And it still does. Weller then asked about the song, almost defensively, 'They're not annoyed about it, are they?'. The answer was no; the Eton schoolboys were buying it as much as the rest of us, including, one can assume, future Prime Minister David Cameron, when on a Radio 4 programme in 2008, he claimed it was his favourite song:

> I was one, in the corp (the 'corp' being the Eton Rifles). It meant a lot, some of those early Jam albums we used to listen to. I don't see why the left should be the only ones allowed to listen to protest songs.

Weller's reply came in *The New Statesman:*

> Which part of it didn't he get? It wasn't intended as a fucking drinking song for the cadet corps.

Whoever bought the single, and whatever their reasons, it became The Jam's first Top Ten hit and cemented their place in the upper echelons of British bands.

1979 was also the year of the Mod revival in the UK, which spawned a myriad of bands, some good, some not so good, some bloody awful, and The Jam generally – and Weller in particular – were deemed responsible, if that's the right word. It must also be said the feature film based on The Who album *Quadrophenia* also helped propel the movement.

Although Weller would constantly deny 'ownership' of the movement, the clothes, the guitars and the songs they chose to cover made it difficult for them to distance themselves. It would become a bone of contention for Weller in the years that followed, especially when the violence associated with the original mods manifested itself in the new mods and, particularly, at Jam gigs, which should have been celebratory affairs but, as I've noted, often had a worrying air of malevolence in and around the venues.

'Heatwave' (Holland, Dozier, Holland)

When, in 1963, Martha and the Vandellas skipped across the nation's turntable with this swingin' soul number, its airy, syncopated rhythm filled the dancefloors, the kids' feet barely touching the floor such is its lightness of touch. In the hands of The Jam, it's a full-on, breathless stampede towards the end of the album. Attempting to add the lightness that the original has in buckets is the piano playing of 'Merton' Mick Talbot, and if ever ivories can be described as 'tinkled' this is as good an example you'll hear on an otherwise steamroller of a track. Essentially, though, it's a throwaway filler and a disappointing end to an album full of musical and lyrical creativity.

'See-Saw' (Weller)

B-side to 'The Eton Rifles'

Opening with a double guitar staccato intro, the song settles into a very '60s mod/pop tune about a relationship that, in the eyes of the teller, has ended far too early. It's a story that's familiar to almost everyone and, in that respect, has the benefit of recognition from the listener:

Your friends told me you moved out of town,
I got your address and I wrote it down,
I used the pen that you bought for my birthday,
And every stroke, you know, reminded me of you,
I realise that we'll never be together again.

With the passing of time, of course, I think an added sadness is that the address would be logged on your phone's address book. And what exactly is a pen? Remind me again.

Surprisingly for a song written by Weller, it's Foxton who opens the vocals, but as the song continues, and Weller and Foxton sing large parts together, it's the song that best showcases how well the two's voices fit together, Weller with the higher, more forceful part, Foxton an altogether calmer, more measured approach. It wouldn't work for every song, but it's perfect here.

'Going Underground' (Weller)

7" double A-side (with 'The Dreams Of Children') cat. no. POSP 113
Also available as a 7" double-pack cat. no. POSPJ 113
Recorded at The Townhouse Studios
Produced by Vic Coppersmith-Heaven
UK release date: 7 March 1980
Highest UK chart position: 1

Opening with a not-unfamiliar combination of staccato guitar and bass, 'Going Underground' introduces itself in an unflinching fashion and is perhaps the Jam 'sound' at its zenith; certainly, no other single after sounded anything like the previous nine.

Arguably Weller's first clearly political song, as in No. 10 politics, (in the video photos of politicians – including Edward Heath, the Harold's MacMillan and Wilson, and Margaret Thatcher – are all swept away in one indignant flash of the hand), it's an attack on society in all its forms, and how the world, with blithe acceptance from the proletariat, has turned into a dangerous place that anyone with a lick of sense would want to hide from:

And the public gets what the public wants,
But I want nothing this society's got,
I'm going underground.

The previous year, the USSR had invaded Afghanistan and the US had responded as it was always going to. Perhaps for the first time since the Cuban missile crisis of 1962, the world appeared to be on the brink of nuclear armageddon. The video, although primarily a simple performance to camera, is nevertheless crammed with imagery, some overt (the Lord Kitchener and Uncle Sam World War One recruitment posters), some less so (the red telephone that was a symbol of the communication line between the US and USSR during the cold war. Tellingly, in the video, the phone is off the hook). Weller tells us that whatever might happen, it's our choice, our fault, that these people are making our decisions:

> You choose your leaders and place your trust,
> As their lies wash you down and their promises rust,
> You'll see kidney machines replaced by rockets and guns.

Musically, the track screams along at pace as Foxton and Buckler push the whole forwards with their by now familiar energy and force, and, in the middle-eight, borrows from 'The Eton Rifles' with a single line Hammond organ fill, and introduces 'la-la-la's', incongruous in the surrounding maelstrom of noise but a lyrical motif that Weller had used before and would visit again. In the style of many of the songs on *Setting Sons*, it is lyrically dense, line after line attacking all and sundry, even at one point the band themselves as, in the video to the track, Weller sings 'these braying sheep on my TV screen', whilst bent over a TV set showing an image of The Jam staring back at him. No one gets off lightly.

> What you see is what you get,
> You've made your bed, you better lie in it.

The Jam's first number-one single happened whilst the band were on tour in America. Having finished a Saturday night gig in Los Angeles, California, Weller, Foxton and Buckler were in the room of their tour manager, Kenny Wheeler, enjoying a few post-gig drinks when the news came from Britain. It shouldn't have been too much of a surprise as Polydor already had 200,000 copies on pre-order, and the marketing department had released the single on Tuesday, rather than the more usual Thursday, giving it extra days to sell before the chart was released on Sunday morning. Despite these tactics – and who is anyone to comment on them, this is the music industry, after all – it seemed inevitable that the band would reach the top spot sooner or later. The previous three years of touring and gathering fans along the way had already paid off with successful releases and with 'The Eton Rifles' reaching number three, who's to say that 'Going Underground' wouldn't have been a number one anyway. That's certainly the way the band thought, and the fans couldn't have cared less. However, there was a problem. The Jam were five and a half thousand miles away. It took less than five minutes for them to decide to finish the US tour early and head back home to appear on *Top Of The Pops*, which was to be recorded the following Wednesday.

For the performance, Weller decided to appear wearing a Heinz tomato soup apron, a nod to pop art and The Who's Roger Daltrey, who was pictured in a bathtub of Heinz baked beans on the cover of the *Sell Out* album. The strictly anti-product placement BBC were unhappy and determined not to allow Weller to wear it. Weller argued the point and finally agreed to wear the apron back-to-front. Find the clip on YouTube and decide for yourself whether the BBC were successful in their attempt to stifle such blatant advertising.

From a purely fashionista perspective, and what's mod without the fashion element, in both the video and *Top Of The Pops* performance, Weller wears a Tootal scarf. This became an easy way out for those who couldn't be arsed to make the effort. Wear a Tootal scarf over your normal clothes and be a mod for the night. And yes, I do own a Tootal scarf, but I always made the effort.

To cash in on The Jam's burgeoning popularity, Polydor re-released all nine of the band's previous singles, six of which charted. This gave the band the most singles in one chart since The Beatles over a decade earlier. Little by little, Weller's dream of being 'bigger than The Beatles' was gaining momentum.

As an aside, and solely to point out the lasting legacy of The Jam, I want to bring to your attention two TV shows. In a 2016 edition of *Travel Man*, the presenter – the writer, actor and director Richard Ayoade – is in Copenhagen with fellow traveller, comedian Noel Fielding. To introduce a piece about the city's metro system, Ayoade's voiceover begins, 'We're going to make like beat combo The Jam and go underground', before this exchange between the companions:

Fielding: Can I be Weller?
Ayoade: No, I don't want to be Bruce Foxton again. I'm always Foxton in our Jam role-play.

Over 30 years after the demise of The Jam, the band can still be the focus of an off-the-cuff dialogue that the producers and director of the show decided had enough resonance with their audience not to hit the cutting room floor. Fast forward to spring 2023 and Sky premiers its cliché-ridden tale of south London villains relocating to the Costa Del Crime in the 1980s. Episode one, scene one, opens to the strains of 'Going Underground' and a blink-and-you-miss-it cameo of Paul Weller, giving tacit approval of the show. The show's title? *A Town Called Malice*. You just can't keep a good band down.

'The Dreams Of Children' (Weller)
7" double A-side (with Going Underground) cat. no. POSP 113
Also available as a 7" double-pack cat. no. POSPJ 113
Recorded at The Townhouse Studios
Produced by Vic Coppersmith-Heaven

UK release date: 7 March 1980
Highest UK chart position: 1
Opening with a backwards snippet of 'Thick As Thieves' and repeated throughout the song in what, as Weller jokingly called it, 'our west-coast phase', 'The Dreams Of Children' was intended to be an A-side in its own right but a mistake at the pressing plant also made 'Going Underground' an A-side and radio DJs, given the choice, decided the solid Jam sound of the latter more radio-friendly fodder for the Jam fanbase.

Although it might have shown a little more experimentation musically, it's still clearly The Jam; the springy guitar riff rolling into choppy chords, the repeating pounding rhythm of the bass and the hold-it-all-together tightness of Buckler's drums. On the face of it, you might expect the dreams of children to be rainbows, unicorns and fluffy things, but we're soon disabused of that:

I sat alone with the dreams of children,
Weeping willows and tall dark buildings and,
I've caught a fashion from the dreams of children,
But woke up sweating to this modern nightmare.

In the hands of Weller, and echoing the bleak future that is set before us on this flip side:

I woke up to a grey and lonely picture,
The streets below left me feeling dirty.

There's a breakdown that introduces a light, breezy organ for a few bars before the song pounds back into the riff and we're off again.

I fell in love with the dreams of children,
I saw a vision of all the happy days,
I've caught a fashion from the dreams of children,
But woke up sweating from this modern nightmare.

The song ends with a repeated refrain, 'You will crack on your dreams tonight', as the music collapses with Buckler's skittish snare and a plaintive organ playing a looping riff until the fade out.

The video has some outdoor scenes, and the beaten-up playground the band play on under gloomy skies is suitably depressing. At one point, though, with Weller and Buckler in the foreground, breath misty due to the cold, Foxton stands away in the distance and suddenly starts waving like an excited child. It's a strange image. The indoor scenes were obviously filmed at the same time as 'Going Underground', but studio lighting has been added giving the whole thing a feeling of artifice, obvious because we're watching a video but usually not shown in the finished product. There's an attempt at some avant-garde, deconstructivism as we see a mic stand without a mic for Foxton and a mic 'floating' for Weller (I say floating, but the wires are quite visible at times, or is this the point?) There's a red-lined opera cloak, a top hat on the floor and a glass bust with what appears to be a yellow splodge of brains inside. If these are the dreams that children have, their parents need to stop feeding them cheese at night time.

Bonus 7" single released with the first 100,000 copies.
'Away From The Numbers' (Weller), **'The Modern World'** (Weller), **'Down In The Tube Station At Midnight'** (Weller)
All three tracks were recorded at the Rainbow Theatre in London on 3 November 1979. The recordings have little to add to The Jam's legacy except that, as an inducement to fans to pre-order 'Going Underground', it helped project the single to number one in the hit parade, where it stayed for three weeks. The single was also the first to enter the chart at the top since Slade in 1973 with "Merry Xmas Everybody'. It's true that the Slade single gets more annual radio plays than The Jam's single, but it's also true that The Jam single is better than the Slade single by as many Christmases as you can imagine.

Boy, It's A Tough, Tough World – Sound Affects To Funeral Pyre

Sound Affects

LP cat. no. POLD 5025
Recorded at The Townhouse Studios, London
Produced by Vic Coppersmith-Heaven and The Jam
UK release date: 28 November 1980
Highest UK chart placing: 2

Recording for the band's fifth album began after they returned from touring in America. Weller had been exploring the poetry of Percy Shelly and had been reading *Camelot And The Vision Of Albion* by historian and Arthurian expert Geoffrey Ash, which Weller counted as a major influence on his writing at the time. *Sound Affects* was another set of songs that Weller was being pressured into writing, nothing new there, but here, at last, he was enjoying the process more. Many of the songs were written in the studio from scratch or taking ideas from Foxton and Buckler's jamming. The entire feel of the album is a sideways step from what the band had produced before. Gone is the mountain of overdubs that were such a feature of *Setting Sons*, to be replaced by a more sparse and spiky sound. The Jam have never made any secret of their influences and would be happy to nick ideas if they felt it would enhance a record. With this in mind, whilst The Jam were in the studio for *Sound Affects*, another very English band, XTC, were recording down the corridor and Rick Buckler made this comment on XTC's drummer, Terry Chambers, 'There was plenty to be inspired by.' Whether there is a great deal of influence is down to the listener, but it's true that nothing happens in isolation.

Although this stripped-down sound gave the songs a more immediate feel, the pace of recording was numbingly slow. The Jam were about immediacy and not worrying too much about rough edges, but that wasn't the Coppersmith-Heaven way. After three months in the studio, and a whopping £120,000 spent, the band were happy with the songs but not the production, despite The Jam having a production credit on the album sleeve. It was the last time the band recorded with Coppersmith-Heaven.

Despite the band being dissatisfied with the result, the critics once again applauded the album. Paul Du Noyer in the *NME* recognised The Jam's need for constant change,

This album takes the band forward ... it's a brave departure and an earnest effort to break new ground ... instrumentation is stark, spare and hard ... where *Sound Affects* is good, it's great, and where it's not so good, it's still good.

In *Sounds,* Dave McCullough reminded us why The Jam had ridden the punk, new wave and mod fashions and come out the other side stronger:

86

The fact that Paul Weller talks to ordinary people in an extraordinary voice but minus the usual deceit and malice … (his) humanism is as simple and direct as it is unaffected … he cares.

In *Melody Maker*, a music paper not always wholly taken by The Jam, Patrick Humphries wrote of the album:

It's flawed, but even in those flaws lie the seeds for the future, fascinating developments… Weller has set himself impressively high standards and *Sound Affects* does not fully realise his capabilities … while I admire this album, I do not like it. Not yet.

I wonder if Patrick has come around to it by now?

Finally, in the *Record Mirror*, Mike Gardner finds time to point out, albeit in an offhand kind of way, that The Jam is more than one person:

(Regarding) the ability, talent and maturity of Paul Weller … his acute ear for melody, his instinctive feel for the right emotional tinting, his powerful and relentless, and mental and physical attack are the seeds brought to fruition by the drive of his rhythm section cohorts.

'Rhythm section cohorts'? I suppose even being mentioned is something.

The album sleeve design is taken from a run of albums of sound effects released by the BBC through the 1970s. The sort where track one is 'door being slammed', track two is 'footsteps on a gravel path', and so on. The images on *Sound Affects* relate in some way to the tracks on the album, so we have a police car, a pound sign and discarded frozen packages (fish fingers, peas and ice cream to be accurate). The rear of the sleeve has some verses from Percy Shelley's *Mask Of Anarchy*, which much like a lot of the band's output, was written as a call to the masses:

Rise like lions after slumber,
In unvanquishable number,
Shake your chains to earth like dew,
Which in sleep had fallen on you,
Ye are many, they are few.

(A few years later, when I was at night school, earning credits to belatedly go to university, I stole these verses as part of an exercise the class had been set to write a 'stirring speech' for a politician to rouse the electorate to vote. My tutor was impressed and asked if I liked the work of Shelley. I said, 'Nah, Paul Weller'.)

The inside sleeve had the lyrics as we'd by now come to expect but in full as one of the tracks is an instrumental and so space wasn't an issue. It's also the first album not to have a cover version. The reverse of the inside sleeve is an atmospheric, early morning shot of the band on the edge of a pond with a country house in the background, as far away from the urban grit of the first two albums as you can imagine and certainly more likely to conjure 'visions of Albion'.

'Pretty Green' (Weller)

Touted as a single by Polydor (indeed, artwork for the sleeve had already been produced before Weller insisted on 'Start!'), 'Pretty Green' opens the band's fifth album with a single-note bassline, which, when played live and extended, had the crowds bouncing up and down long before the drums and guitar kicked in. The creation of the song had begun with Foxton and Buckler playing around with ideas in the recording studio before Weller added a simple yet bitingly effective lyric. The spareness of the music, much like that in 'Tube Station', allowed the lyrics to be clearly heard and was markedly different to the at times suffocating denseness of *Setting Sons*.

As might be imagined from the title, the song is an attack on the Thatcherite money obsession that overwhelmed Britain in the 1980s and has never really gone away, and how real knowledge is as likely to come from the street as from formal education.

> And they didn't teach me that in school,
> It's something that I've learnt on my own,
> That power is measured by the pound or the fist,
> It's as clear as this.

The song is stark in its musical simplicity and direct in its lyrics, it tells its story and it gets out of there:

> This is the pretty green, this is society,
> You can't do nothing unless it's in the pocket, oh no.

'Monday' (Weller)

Despite the number of love songs that Weller had produced it was 'Monday' where he finally laid his cards on the table, 'I will never be embarrassed about love again'. Fuelled by a top string, high-in-the-mix bassline and skittish drums, it plays with vaguely psychedelic musical themes and has a nice piano addition that tumbles down the chord sequence towards the end of the track. Weller's delivery has real longing and yearning as he stretches for the high notes. There's a true poetic feel to the lyric, too; although perhaps erring occasionally on the side of melodrama, the plaintive call for love is clear to hear:

> Rainclouds came and stole my thunder,
> Left me barren, like a desert.

Although The Jam were by now the number one band in the country (I was going to add 'arguably' but I'm not, they were, no argument), they had always considered themselves down-to-earth people, always keeping a connection with the fans, letting them into soundchecks and signing countless autographs and answering countless questions, and Weller addresses this as he sings:

> Tortured winds that blew me over,
> When I start to think that I'm something special,
> They tell me that I'm not,
> And they're right and I'm glad that I'm not.

Try telling the army of Jam fans that Weller wasn't special, and you'd get a very different answer. It's remarkable that the band, and Weller in particular, managed to keep their feet on the ground throughout this period of their career.

'But I'm Different Now' (Weller)
We're back on familiar ground. A furious guitar intro, Foxton with an above-the-twelfth fret 'woo-woo', and Buckler furiously attacking the sixteenths on the hi-hat. It's as thrashy as anything on *In The City* but played with the musical dexterity the band as individuals had been growing into at an almost exponential rate. Lyrically, we're in the same love song territory as 'Monday', but here, Weller admits his mistakes and takes all the blame:

> Because I know I done some things,
> That I should never have done,
> But I'm different now and I'm glad that you're my girl.

And in a very 1960s one minute and 50 seconds later, it's all over.

'Set The House Ablaze' (Weller)
Coming in at, for a Jam song, a colossal five minutes, 'Set The House Ablaze' is Weller's tirade against the injustice inherent in society. There's more Orwellian language – 'indoctrination' is not a word that crops up on many songs – and there are also nods to his growing belief that The Jam were failing to have the impact he was hoping for. Not in relation to album sales and the nebulous concept of 'stardom' (it would likely be called 'celebrity' today) but on the fans who hung on his every word, yet obviously failing to heed them.

> I think we've lost our perception,
> I think we've lost sight of the goals we should be working for.

Before earnestly hoping to find an answer:

> I wish that there was something I could do about it,
> I wish that there was some way I could try to fight it,
> Scream and shout it.

The track begins with Weller picking a riff on a minor chord (slightly unusual as minor chords tend to be used on love songs as they give a more mellow sound than the corresponding major chord, and, as the title of the song suggests, this is no mellow love song) until Foxton and Buckler crash in and the whole thing pushes along on four-to-the-floor snare. Weller repeats the same riff over the opening verses, giving a feeling of claustrophobia, very *Setting Sons* but not very *Sound Affects*, which never leaves the song. And then there's the whistling.

With different instrumentation being introduced into the band's sound, trumpets could easily have played this riff, therefore, we can assume the whistling is used to make a point. Whistling may be a staple of folk songs or a riff to toot if you're leaving old Durham town, but it's unexpectedly layered on top of an aggressive attack on neo-Nazism, though to me, the sound does recall parades of uniformed men and boys, boots crunching in strict unison. (The right arm raised at a 100 degree-ish angle is optional.)

Much of the inspiration for the song came from Geoffrey Ashe's *Camelot and the Vision of Albion*, and Britain – or specifically England, as written about by Weller, particularly in the opening stages of his career – as a land for heroes that has been ruthlessly and ignominiously brought to its knees by successive political hatchet men and women. (As I write, Britain is no longer on its knees, it is prostrate.)

Although the song itself is a powerful, spirited addition to the band's canon, what I find disappointing is the drop-down towards the end. We've already discovered how important lyrics are to Weller and the spoken element here is so far back in the mix it's difficult to pick out the opening stanza – though thoughtfully reproduced on the inside sleeve of the album – and all but impossible to understand the second, which isn't written down. Assuming that at the time, this was done for a reason, with the release of so many of The Jam's songs in pointlessly remixed form since (see: *Extras*) as a fan and someone who took Weller's lyrics seriously, it would have been nice to have them front and centre.

'Start!' (Weller)
7" cat no. 2059 266
Recorded at The Townhouse Studios, London
Produced by Vic Coppersmith-Heaven and The Jam
UK release date: 15 August 1980
Highest UK chart position: 1

'It's exactly the same as 'Taxman'', was the cry from all and sundry when 'Start!' first hit the radio stations. It would be ridiculous to try to avoid the comparison (how does the saying go, 'imitation is the sincerest form of flattery') with Foxton's 'imitation' of McCartney's bass line, and Weller's chopped chords and spiky backwards guitar, infused psychedelic solo. However, taking the song as a whole, the differences matter more than the similarities, though the video does little to dampen the Beatle accusations. Filmed in a cramped setting, Buckler wearing headphones as someone would in a recording studio, the video focused on the music (though the camera operator throws in some wild, swinging angles, very 1960s.) Weller dons a pair of round sunglasses akin to those worn by George Harrison and Paul McCartney on the back cover of *Revolver* (homage, imitation or just plain stealing? Frankly, who cares?) and plays his pop-art Rickenbacker high on his chest, unlike his usual style, but very much in the Harrison mould.

Lyrically, whereas Harrison was complaining of the startlingly high 95% 'supertax' rate imposed by Harold Wilson's Labour Government on the UK's highest earners, Weller turns his attention to the Spanish Civil War. He'd been reading George Orwell for some time and Orwell's recollections of his time fighting the fascists in Spain, *Homage To Catalonia*, where he joined one of the International Brigades, groups made up of non-Spanish people from around the world who could barely communicate with each other, inform the idea and lyrics of 'Start!':

It's not important for you to know my name,
Nor I to know yours,
If we communicate for two minutes only,
It will be a start.

The feelings of togetherness and solidarity that only a shared experience can instil resonated with Weller.

The single sleeve is a plain dark pink colour with 'Start!' written across the bottom. It was only the third single that had no photo of the band, and the group failed to appear on each subsequent 7" sleeve. Given that the band had been 'cover stars' since the beginning of their career with Polydor, anyone who had an ounce of knowledge of the British music scene at the time would have recognised The Jam. As early as 1977, they'd been on the front of the *NME, Melody Maker* and *Sounds* and by the time 'Start!' was released, they'd progressed to the more 'teen' magazines such as *Smash Hits* and *Supersonic*. The need for their pictures to be on record sleeves to help people identify the band was long past. The rear of the sleeve has an aerial view of a turntable that looks very 1960s, as if the record needed any more '60s references.

The publicity artwork has a 1920s pseudo-Russian feel, with its drawings of factories and hammers and good comrades, which brings to mind another of Orwell's novels, *1984*. Although Polydor wanted 'Pretty Green' to be the single to follow 'Going Underground' Weller, as pugnacious as ever, insisted on 'Start!' and he was proved right as the single became the band's second consecutive number one.

On the *Sound Affects* album, the song has an extended coda, with horn stabs and some off-beat drums, while Foxton pumps away with his unchanging bass line, but it adds little to the song and it's certainly better in its shorter version.

'That's Entertainment' (Weller)
7" German import released on the Metronome label cat. no. 0030 364
B-side 'Down In The Tube Station At Midnight' (live) (Weller)
Release date: 30 January 1981
Highest UK chart position: 21
Side one ends with 'That's Entertainment', which was never released as a single in the UK but, such was the popularity of the band, enough were sold on German import to chart at number 21.

There are so many brilliant images of contemporary life in the lyrics that it would take far too long to discuss them all, and so I'll leave you to (re-) discover them for yourselves. Musically, it's a four-chord repeating acoustic strum, with a trademark walking bassline and a masterclass of what not to play as a drummer. The falsetto harmonies and backward guitars help shift the song into other areas as the basic melody never alters, not even a key change that so subtly shifts the dynamic of 'English Rose'. On the compilation album *Snap!*, there is a demo version of the song which, the sleeve notes announce, 'although technically not as good as the later version... the demo has a certain quality that was never captured again.' Although musically speaking, I would personally always choose a sound that is not technically good over something that has been produced to within an inch of its life, the demo version, with its scratchy single acoustic guitar, a plod-plod-plod bassline that simply plays the root note of the chords and a straight four-four drumbeat, does the song no justice at all.

Weller refers to the tune on the sleeve notes of the live album *Dig The New Breed*, 'Coming home from the pub and writing 'That's Entertainment' in 10 minutes. 'Weller's finest song to date'. Hah!' In fact, as we've seen, the germ of the idea had been around for a while from Paul Drew's poem, *Entertainment*, published on Weller's *Riot Stories* label.

'Dream Time' (Weller)
Opening side two is a track that most people thought was called 'Supermarket' due to the word being repeated throughout the song. In fact, 'Dream Time' is one of very few songs in the Jam canon that doesn't include the song title in its lyric.

It wasn't the first time that Weller had used a supermarket as a metaphor for modern life (see: 'In The Crowd'), but I would argue that he'd never done it better than with 'Dream Time'. It's another dystopian future (Orwell has a lot to answer for) and Weller has never sounded so panicked as he delivers line after line drenched in fear,

Scared I was, sweating now,
Feeling of doom, my bowels turned to water.

But the chorus soars and, for a moment, allows us a glimpse of what might be before bringing us crashing back to earth:

I saw the lights and the pretty girls and I,
Thought to myself what a pretty world but there's,
Something else here that puts me off.

Abruptly, mid-way, the song slams on the brakes, Foxton loops a bass line and Weller, as though waking from the dream, at least sees the way out:

Boy, it's a tough, tough world,
But you've got to be tough with it.

To ram home his conclusion, 'tough with it', is repeated 13 times (and although I'd like to make reference to 'unlucky for some' and the bleakness of existence, I think the truth is that it fits in the chord structure and number of bars), the first seven with Buckler rolling around the toms giving a sense of unending foreboding, and then the last half dozen, Weller straining in falsetto, and Buckler in double-time snare hits, each line accentuated with guitar and horns stabbing with nascent fury.

I'm so scared dear,
My love comes in frozen packs.

It's a very Jam kind of song; a full sound, the guitars are very much back into the mix, playing around with arrangements and lots of backing vocals, and was based around an idea that Foxton and Buckler had altered slightly to fit with a Weller melody.

Before the explosion of sound that is the start of the tune, there are 45 seconds of ambient sound; all backwards recording and the haunting voice of a woman. The reason for this rather bemusing intro? No idea, to be honest, except it lulls the listener into a false sense of security as to what's going to happen next, musically speaking, though the dreamy nature of the sounds fits both with the song title and the photo on the inside sleeve of the album.

There is a grainy video of sorts for 'Dream Time' that begins with shots of random British scenes of very depressing, ugly streets. It then cuts to the same studio as the *Start!* video, the band wearing the same outfits and playing the same guitars. It's done with one camera, no cuts and feels and looks very much like a last-minute idea, 'just in case'.

'Man In The Corner Shop' (Weller)
More social comment from Weller, this time from the point of view of three individuals, though not our friends from *Setting Sons*; the factory boss (though not the owner, he'd like to have his own factory), the customer (working at the factory, who would like to be his own boss) and the titular corner shop owner, who, despite his 'hard life' is content to be his own boss.

If that makes the song sound complicated, it's really anything but. The number came together quickly. Weller: 'I made it up on the spot at a rehearsal one day. I had some lyrics already, but I made the chords up out of thin air'.

Weller called the song 'really English' and the lyrics described each character with their own dreams as, 'all one big unnecessary struggle'.

Puts up the closed sign does the man in the corner shop,
Serves his last then he says goodbye to him,
He knows it is a hard life,
But it's nice to be your own boss, really.
Walks off home does the last customer,
He is jealous of the man in the corner shop,
He's sick of working at the factory,
Says it must be nice to be your own boss, really.

A typical falling chord sequence of guitar opens the number, Foxton and Buckler join in and the song rolls along, ending with sing-along 'la, la, la's. Before we reach the end, however, Weller reminds us that, whatever our position in life might be, there is one place where society and its mores are immaterial:

Go to church do the people from the area,
All shapes and classes sit and pray together,
For here they are all one,
For God created all men equal.

It's quite a stretch to say that, in 1981, our friends would all be in church together (though, being a secular kind of person, I really wouldn't know), though it doesn't hurt to remember that, despite what God might think, some men are more equal than others.

'Music For The Last Couple' (Weller, Foxton, Buckler)
Usually, when a band enters a rehearsal room, or even a studio for that
matter, there is a kind of warm-up period. The drummer loosens up, the bass
and guitar players get their fingers moving. Sometimes, someone will have
an idea they've been working on and so a loose jam begins to see if anything
can come of it, though as often as not, it merely sounds like a souped-up
version of an orchestra tuning before a concert. Eventually, let's say after 15
or 20 minutes, someone will suggest doing something of use. The problem is,
if no one makes that suggestion, and you're a professional band recording an
album that's a track or two short, you record the jumble of rhythms and half-
baked ideas, give it a title and release it. Containing only one lyric; 'I think
of boats and trains and all those things that make you want to get away', the
song is the only track to have a whole band songwriting credit. Which is a
shame for Buckler.

'Boy About Town' (Weller)
After the turgid plod of 'Music For The Last Couple' something was needed to
blast the cobwebs away. 'Boy About Town' is a punchy, two-minute rush of
working-class optimism:

See me walking around I'm the boy about town that you heard of.
See me walking the streets I'm on top of the world that you heard of.

Though tinged with Weller's inescapable touch of melancholy, 'There's more
than you can hope for in this world'.
    Without trying at all, this 1960s tight little pop number carries the listener
away and harks back to the heady days of the early mods when you could
afford a suit and a scooter, albeit on the HP. 'Na-na-na-na's replace lyrics at
the bridge and an enthusiastic horn section lifts the whole song towards its
rousing end.

'Scrape Away' (Weller)
Much like the songs ending *All Mod Cons*, where you were uplifted with 'The
Place I Love' before being dragged back to earth with ''A'-Bomb' and 'Tube
Station', 'Boy About Town' is followed by 'Scrape Away', a song that feels as
though it's prowling towards you from the shadows. With a slow, pulsating
bassline, off-beat drums and a prickly guitar line, you know this isn't a love
song. Quite the opposite, as the opening line makes abundantly clear:

Your twisted cynicism makes me feel sick,
Your open disgust for idealistic naïve.

And so it goes on, never letting up for a minute in a savage attack on the
businessman (perhaps the businessman who was so scathing on 'Burning Sky'):

What makes once young minds get in this state,
Is it age or just the social climate?
You're talking like some fucking hardened MP,
You're saying power's all, it's power you need!

Starting out like many of the songs on *Sound Affects* as a drum and bass pattern, the track shows what can happen when an unformed idea in itself has enough about it to be moulded into a coherent whole. There are a few studio tricks thrown in on the vocal, which make the track stand out against what, to this point, has been a very live-sounding album. 'Scrape Away' brings *Sound Affects* to a close with a repeated refrain in French, the sort of pretentiousness largely absent from The Jam, but which would come roaring to the fore with The Style Council.

La puissance c'est tout,
C'est la puissance dont tu as besoin.

Spoken by Laurent Locher, singer and guitarist with French mod band Les Lords, who'd had a short-lived career in 1979 and 1980, and translated as 'Power is everything, it's power you need', it's a downbeat sentiment, almost giving in to the people that Weller had railed about throughout The Jam's career. It was another six months before the band released new material.

'Liza Radley' (Weller)
B-side to 'Start!'
It was always going to happen; with the clear nod to 'Taxman' on the A-side of the single, having the title of the B-side as a female's name, the likeness to 'Eleanor Rigby' is too obvious not to state, though the solo work of Syd Barrett can also be heard. Weller described the song as, 'A piece of nonsense... just me playing around being psychedelic, English and whimsical', but there's not a lot of whimsy in Liza's life and her sadness isn't dissimilar to that of Eleanor, of lonely people living outside of what society deems the norm:

The people of the town where we live say,
'She's not quite right, she don't fit in with a small town'.

Played on acoustic guitar, with some interjections by Foxton which mirror the 'Start!'/'Taxman' bass line (Foxton also supplies the accordion), the song ends by telling us that perhaps these outsiders, these people who we shun and laugh at, might know more than we give them credit for.

But no matter what they say, in her mind,
She knows their dream of life,
They won't ever find.

'Funeral Pyre' (Words: Weller, Music: The Jam)
7" cat. no. POSP 257
Recorded at The Townhouse Studios, London
Produced by Pete Wilson and The Jam
UK release date: 29 May 1981
Highest UK chart position:

After six months of radio silence, the band came crashing back with 'Funeral Pyre'. Following the clean and clipped 'Start!' and the sometimes psychedelic musings of *Sound Affects*, 'Funeral Pyre' takes the band in an altogether different area. The single was the first produced by Polydor sound engineer Pete Wilson (though The Jam also get a credit) and the sound is significantly different not only from the previous single but from just about everything else they'd recorded.

I remember thinking at the time the sound was 'muddy', with Buckler barely letting up on snare rolls for the entire song, and Foxton's thundering bassline not giving the song any room to breathe. However, both are necessary to keep the track in some kind of form as Weller slashes away on power chords, sometimes only narrowly sounding in time. Indeed, the entire song sounds as though it could collapse in on itself at any moment.

The lyrics (helpfully printed on the back of the single sleeve) are as aggressive as the music:

Down in among the streets tonight,
Books will burn, people laugh and cry in their turmoil.
We feast on flesh, and drink on blood.

The song is relentless and, released at a time when the new romantics were starting to take over the charts with songs that bore little relation to the lives we were living, shows the wilful bloody-mindedness that Weller had displayed so far in The Jam's career; we're going to write and release whatever we want to.

The single's sleeve buys into the idea of dourness and depression with its stark drawing of naked bodies and dismembered heads. Drawn in shades of black, grey and white, it's as uncompromising as it is unsettling. There is a small reminder of what life could be with a circular photo of a utopian Garden of Eden sitting next to the printed lyrics on the reverse side.

The video for the song took the band back to Woking and the sand pits where H.G. Wells had set the start of the Martian invasion in his 1897 novel *War Of The Worlds*. Whether this site was chosen simply because it was near the band's home, or because of the connection with Wells' book, I don't know, but it's a suitable place. It was filmed at dusk and used local teenagers to play the 'mob'. It's noticeable there are no adults involved (save the band, of course) and it tells us squarely who the song is aimed at. It's a cautionary tale to the youth that Weller had been so enamoured with only a few years previously and warns of succumbing to the disagreeable rhetoric of right-wing racist groups. It tells of mob mentality and the hysteria this can engender. The lyrics are obvious enough but, when seen in tandem with the video, and certainly as far as the arts are concerned, it recalls John Lennon's 'more popular than Jesus' statement, and the public (over)reaction that followed with Beatles records and memorabilia being thrown on pyres across America. That, in turn, leads us to the burning crosses in the American South and, if anyone had still missed the point, the video includes two snippets of contemporary film of the book burnings that took place in Nazi Germany in the 1930s. Weller is telling us to take care not to follow that path because:

> If you get too burnt,
> You can't come back home.

Despite the bellicose music, production and lyrics of the song, it still peaked at number four in the charts. As the previous two singles had both made number one, it could be seen as a relative failure. I would argue the fact that such a song even entered into the Top Ten at all, given the popular musical landscape of the time and the fact that 'Funeral Pyre' ends with a 25-second snare-only drum solo, made it an astonishing success. But it was the last Jam single that featured only the core of the band, and future releases saw them moving away from the power three-piece, adding more instrumentation and guest vocalists and, ultimately, they became, to an extent, a different band.

'Disguises' (Townshend)
B-side to 'Funeral Pyre'
Written by Pete Townshend and appearing as the lead track on The Who's 1966 'Ready, Steady, Who' EP, 'Disguises' was the second song that The Jam covered from the release, the first being 'Batman' on *In The City*.

From start to finish, this is an almost exact copy of The Who's version. The melody – including the key change to introduce the last verse, which is the first verse repeated – the music, the arrangement and even the running time, which is only a few seconds out. The only real difference is that John Entwistle's original French horn solo is replaced by studio effects involving reverb and echo. It's perfunctory at best, and a disappointment from a band whose B-sides had gained a reputation as worthy songs in their own right.

'Absolute Beginners' (Weller)
7" cat. no. POSP 350
Recorded at The Townhouse Studios, London
Produced by Pete Wilson and The Jam
UK release date: 16 October 1981
Highest UK chart position: 4

After the lyrical and musical density of 'Funeral Pyre', 'Absolute Beginners' is positively light-hearted. Coming in with a Stax-inspired horn riff that dominates, the song rushes along at a steady pace but without the guts that Jam fans had come to expect. Indeed, so much did it differ from the Jam 'blueprint' that it gave pause for most fans to wonder about the future development of the band.

Weller, bored with the confines of a three-piece, here began his attempt to turn away from the sound that had brought so much acclaim to become the soul boy he always wanted to be.

The song's title is taken from Colin MacInnes' 1957 novel and eulogy to youth, and although the book's protagonist talks in hep-cat 1950s jazz-inspired lingo, and at one time rides a Vespa and is resolutely not racist, the novel has uncomfortable and violent racist scenes and describes unsavoury racist characters, the sort of character that in reality was becoming more visible as the years and decades passed.

Lyrically, the song is confused, one-liners taking the place of the type of coherent storytelling that was by now Weller's stock-in-trade, but it still reflected his career-long desire for individuals to take control of their own lives and not accept what society was offering:

I lost some hours thinking of it,
I need the strength to go and get what I want.

And in amongst the confused thinking, the end game is always the same:

Come see the tyrants panic, see their crumbling empires fall,
Then tell 'em we don't fight for fools 'cause love is in our hearts!

It's easy to read too much into lyrics and accompanying videos (you've probably noticed by now my tendency to do just that), and with the launching of MTV in August of 1981, everyone now needed a video, but 'Absolute Beginners' opens with the band standing with their backs to each other before sprinting off in different directions. Perhaps the band were at a crossroads (it's actually a give-way at a T junction, but bear with me) and the way forward for Weller was without the constraints that a three-piece brought with them.

The video differs from standard Jam fare as it's the first time there are extended scenes of the band doing something other than simply playing their respective instruments, though it amounts to little more than running down the middle of car-lined streets; Foxton at quite a lick, Buckler more middle-paced and Weller running like a carthorse with cramp. At one point, the band leap out of dry ice for no obvious reason and, later in the track, it's the same leap but rolled backwards and you ask yourself, is this the best that was on offer in 1981? The performance, lots of white and often bleached out, looks pretty cool. Buckler at one juncture in the proceedings, smashes a clock with a spanner, presumably to metaphorically stop time (the end shot is of said clock, smashed beyond repair) as Weller worries, 'time rushed onward without me'. Though this particular scene complements the lyrics, the song's dependency on instrumentation other than guitar, bass and drums foreshadowed what was to come and, in effect, was the beginning of the end for the band.

Before we leave guitars behind, and perhaps only of interest to guitar players, on *Top Of The Pops* from 22 October, Weller played a very rare Rickenbacker 360f (current asking price of around £14,000), whilst a week or so later on 1 November, introduced by the tiresome Noel Edmonds for the BBC children's show *Swap Shop*, he had his very recognisable Rickenbacker 330 pop art 'wham!' guitar. Weller was nothing if not stylish. To my mind, the *Swap Shop* appearance is notable for Weller's uncharacteristically enthusiastic miming performance. Doing it for the kids, man!

'Tales From The Riverbank' (Weller)
B-side to 'Absolute Beginners'
A very English title for a very English type of psychedelia. After years of writing about the city, the energy of the city, the people in the city that give the city its energy and the place where you need to be to be really alive, Weller takes a sharp left turn to the pastoral musings of 'pastel fields', 'water meadows' and 'a golden country'. It's certainly a more mellow Weller in this unapologetic elegy to the past.

> True it's a dream mixed with nostalgia,
> But it's a dream that I'll always hang on to.

That nostalgia was immediately invoked for people of a certain age who remembered the BBC children's programme of the 1960s and 1970s, the similarly titled *Tales Of The Riverbank*, with its anthropomorphised hamsters, guinea pigs and rats, giving voices to tell their tales as they skittered along a riverbank (the clue is in the title).

In its own way, the TV show was as psychedelic as The Jam's song. The track itself fades in with the circular guitar line running note for note in tandem with the bass line and is at the same time haunting and comforting:

> It's mixed with happiness, its mixed with tears,
> Both life and death are carried in this stream,
> That open space you could run for miles.

In the end, Weller is clear about how life is, and who we naturally become as we grow older:

> Now life is so critical, life is too cynical,
> We lose our innocence, we lose our very soul.

Hardly any wonder that, along with its A-side, the single was both a surprise and a puzzle to fans who might have expected, and more than likely wanted, The Jam sound. But there's one thing The Jam never did and that's stay static. Whenever they were in danger of feeling musically constrained the band would veer off, leaving both critics and fans to wonder what might come next.

PAUL WELLER'S TEN GUITARISTS

Left: Circa. 1981. Stuart Adamson's post-Skids band Big Country supported The Jam at Wembley Arena during 1981's Beat Surrender tour. Viv Albertine of The Slits at number six is a real curveball.

1. **Wilko Johnson**
"My first real influence of the '70s."
2. **Pete Townshend (his '65 work)**
"My second and most overwhelming."
3. **Stuart Adamson of The Skids**
4. **Eddie Phillips of The Creation**
"Great effects with feedback and violin bow."
5. **Syd Barrett (his '67 work)**
"Crazy playing."
6. **Viv Albertine of The Slits**
7. **Steve Marriott**
"His playing on all the Small Faces' records. He used a mixture of Steve Cropper and Pete Townshend."
8. **Dave Davies of The Kinks ('64-'69)**
9. **The guitar work on 'Revolver' by The Beatles**
10. **Myself.**
"I enjoy my style and it's exciting to think there's so much more to learn."

Right: Tour dates from the *A Solid Bond In Your Heart* tour in 1982. Were you there?

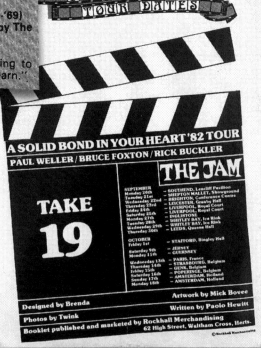

Above: Remember to tick with VHS or Betamax. You wouldn't want to receive the wrong format.

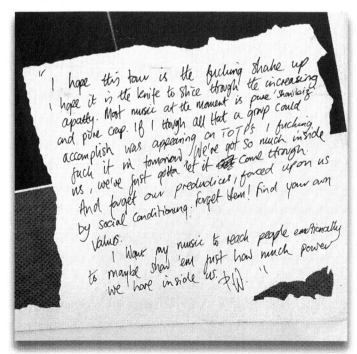

Left: Weller's notes from the *Trans Global Express* tour programme, March and April 1982. 'If I thought all that a group could accomplish was appearing on *TOTP*, I('d) fucking jack it in tomorrow'. As it was, he waited until the end of the year.

103

I'd Better Try Another Brand Pretty Quick – The Gift To Beat Surrender

The Gift

LP cat. no. POLD 5055
Recorded at AIR Studios, London
Produced by Pete Wilson
UK release date: 12 March 1982
Highest UK chart placing: 1
Guest musicians:
Keith Thomas: saxophone
Steve Nichol: trumpet and keyboards
Pete Wilson: keyboards
Russ Henderson: steel drums

The Gift was recorded on either side of Christmas 1981 with a new producer in the seat, Pete Wilson. Weller had worked with Wilson since 1980, though only on demos, and Wilson's speedier way of working appealed to Weller after the time-heavy Coppersmith-Heaven. The recording, however, turned out to be a fraught process, Weller pushing his bandmates and himself hard to create what he thought would be the band's best album, and before long, Weller was arguing with the new producer over the sound:

I really wanted to put everything we had into the LP. I wanted it to be really, really important, and I think I drove it a little bit too hard.

To relax after a day in the studio, Weller was drinking too much and the inevitable happened when, whilst in the studio, he had what has been described as 'a mini breakdown': 'I just felt detached. I felt as if I was in a dream and that I would slip away and not be able to get back'.

Heeding this worrying sign, Weller quit drinking and focused all his energies on the album. However, friction was never far away, with Weller saying some of his demos were better than the finished version. I would say, if you listen to the demos on the *Extras* album, Weller is deluding himself and with that attitude, the only thing that's going to happen is that you'll antagonise your bandmates. But the album came together, and the songs capture the old and new Jam, the power trio and the soulsters (along with British jazz-funk band Pigbag, Weller had said how he was influenced by Spandau Ballet's 'Chant No. 1', calling it 'a genuine British soul record'), though it's this desire to cover all the bases that leaves *The Gift* having less coherence than any of their previous albums except perhaps for *Modern World*.

Again, the critics are roundly in favour whilst still seeing the problems inherent in The Jam; when a band cares so much, it can act as a weight pulling you down. Adam Sweeting in *Melody Maker*:

Weller is virtually alone in this wonderful world of pop in conspicuously giving a damn... the effort nearly cripples him at times.

In the *Record Mirror,* Mark Cooper noted what had made the band what they were was their relentless need to move forward:

The best Jam songs mix an angry kitchen-sink realism with a surging desire for a change ... The Jam have retained their identity while enlarging it to include ringing brass work and best of all, a bubbly happiness.

Graham Lock in the *NME* shows concern for what he sees as The Jam trying to reconcile too many musical differences within a single record:

Though (*The Gift's*) purpose is laudable, it's undermined by a failure to balance questions of style ... he seems tired of the old-style Jam music but knows of no better alternative, so ends up dabbling ... sadly the complexities and rich social detail that went into *All Mod Cons* and *Setting Sons* have largely been ditched ... The Jam have tried too hard to do too much without really having any stronger foundations than their own desperate desire to 'keep movin'.

In *Sounds*, Mick Sinclair is effusive about the album but hits a real note of caution at the end, a note that Weller had already been thinking to himself:

Paul Weller writes and composes because he is a natural social commentator, a talented musician and emotionally articulate ...*The Gift* is another brilliant Jam album. It will be bought in droves and treasured by fans. Thousands will hear it, but how many will actually listen?

Weller's concern about the band's fan base had been apparent for some time and his continued disappointment over the intransigence of the band's core audience (they had booed and heckled support acts Bananarama and The Questions at The Jam's 1980 Christmas concerts) became another addition on Weller's growing list of reasons to end the group.

The album's artwork points to Weller's desire to push the soulful side of the band with the inside sleeve showing a northern soul dancer in mid-air, flares to the full. It also gives the band's new brass section of Keith Thomas and Steve Nichol equal billing (it was the only time that other musicians appeared on any Jam artwork), their photos being the same size as Weller, Foxton and Buckler's, as well as appearing on the live shot on the back of the album's sleeve. (For those who like to read conspiracies into these things, the shot of the band sees Foxton and Buckler almost taking up the same space, with Weller a long way away on the other side of the stage. Is this Weller telling us something we didn't know at the time? Or is it just an album sleeve and Thomas and Nichol needed to be in the shot?)

The front cover sees the band, the three of them, as individuals, the pictures taken on the roof of Air Studios, and if they look awkward, it's because they're literally running on the spot, which was an image Weller had particularly wanted for the cover. Originally, the three photos had a jagged line around them, but Weller was unhappy with the way it looked. The Jam's then-A&R man Dennis Munday told how Weller came to Polydor's offices one morning whilst the sleeve was at the printers and said he really didn't like it. Munday said fine and had 75,000 copies destroyed. That Weller was so invested in the sleeve can be understood as he was credited with design and art direction. When your name is so closely linked to something you're going to worry about the details.

As a fan always looking to be there first when a new piece of Jam vinyl was released, it was a thrill to find initial copies of the album came with its own pink and white striped paper bag. It doesn't sound much, but at the time, these small additions to the standard package gave a shiver of excitement. Forty years on, my bag is a little tattered and a little torn but it's still in one piece.

'Happy Together' (Weller)

And now for those of you watching in black and white,
This one is in technicolour.

Weller opens the band's sixth and final album with these spoken words, a reversal of how the BBC would warn viewers, during the infancy of colour television, not to adjust their colour set as the next programme was meant to be in black and white. Why did Weller choose this beginning? Maybe he was telling the band's fans that this album would be a joyous thing after the dark cynicism that *Sound Affects* is laced with. And indeed, 'Happy Together' would suggest just that, as Foxton shouts 'BABY!' and begins with a thumping bass line leading into a straight four/four northern soul stomp (for the most part, that is, the middle eight takes off in entirely another direction before returning to the pulsating heartbeat of the track). For fans, it was The Jam of old – no trumpets, no piano, no organ – three instruments making a big noise and Weller and Foxton back trading lines in R&B call and response.

The lyric sees Weller in a self-reflective mood, acknowledging the damage he's inflicted on relations and determined to set it straight:

Thought that I was a devil?
But I'm an angel waiting for my wings.
And I was out to hurt you?
But I've no wish to ever cause you pain,
Cos there's enough in this world of sorrow,
I've no wish to add some more to it.

Admirable sentiments, though there's a small shudder that runs through you as the song ends with a very bitter, angry sounding, 'We're happy together, NOW,' the last word spoken in a strangely gruff bark that twists the whole tune and makes you think that perhaps the song isn't quite as sweet as it might seem. Maybe this is Weller's swansong to the legion of Jam fans? Maybe the other songs on the album which are accusatory are also pointed at the fans? Or maybe I'm looking at this from forty years' distance and, like so many others before me, reading too much into it. Again.

'Ghosts' (Weller)

Adam Sweeting in his review of *The Gift* for *Melody Maker,* called 'Ghosts', 'the most haunting and haunted song Weller has ever written'. And he's bang on the money.

A masterclass in restrained drumming, 'Ghosts' opens with picked chords from Weller and a single bass note, anchoring a track that does none of The Jam's ups and downs, ins and outs of melody, musical diversions and left-of-field turns. It lays its cards on the table and doesn't deviate, insistent and driving in its understated way.

In his lyrics, Weller is urging the listener to open up, believe in themselves and have some faith in their own abilities.

Don't live up to your given roles,
There's more inside you that you won't show.

But it's not in any way accusatory, Weller understands that it's a situation that we might all find ourselves in and perhaps we find comfort in being unnoticed, of being invisible:

But you keep it hidden just like everyone,
You're scared to show you care – it'll make you vulnerable.

Throughout Weller's songwriting career, he'd been accused of having the questions but not the answers, something that, generally, he agreed with, arguing that it wasn't his place to provide the answers, but with 'Ghosts' there is a gentle reminder that we're only here once:

One day you'll walk right out of this life,
And then you'll wonder why you didn't try.

And perhaps going for it, whatever 'it' means to you, is worth the risk.

So why are you frightened can't you see that it's you,
At the moment there's nothing so there's nothing to lose,
Lift up your lonely heart and walk right on through.

'Precious' (Weller)

7" double A-side (with 'Town Called Malice') cat. no. POSP 400
12" double A-side (with 'Town Called Malice (live)') cat. no. POSPX 400
Produced by Pete Wilson and The Jam
UK release date: 29 January 1982
Highest UK chart position: 1

When released as a single, 'Precious' was coupled with perhaps the band's most enduring record, 'Town Called Malice'. 'Precious' is a white soul/funk outing that pointed at Weller's new direction more obviously than any other song to date. Buckler introduces the song with sixteenths on the hi-hat, that most disco of rhythms, before Foxton kicks in a slick repeating bass line that he keeps up through the majority of the song.

Although the bass line has Foxton's usual fluidity, it's impossible not to notice the similarity to Pigbag and their 1981 'Papa's Got A Brand New Pigbag' hit single (though the song didn't reach the main UK chart until March of the following year when it peaked at number three after being re-issued). One new style that Foxton did introduce was the 'plucking' of the bass string, acceptable in light of the track being a stab at funk, but otherwise, the pluck has no place in a bass player's armoury. (And neither does the slap, for that matter.) Weller overuses the wah-wah pedal and adds some springy riffs here and there but although the tune swings along and is certainly as danceable a track as any the band had produced, Buckler's thump-thump-thump kick drum makes the whole thing, well, ploddy.

There is some poetic imagery showing Weller at his most love-lorn:

Lonely as the moors on a winter's morning,
Quiet as the sea on a good calm night,
In your tranquil shadow I try and follow.

But, unlike most Jam songs, the lyrics take a back seat to the music.

Pushing this unexpected, and to many Jam fans, unnecessary and even unwanted, foray into white soul was the high-in-the-mix brass, played by Steve Nichol and Keith Thomas. Nichol and Thomas had joined the band on stage towards the end of 1981 when The Jam played some benefit shows for CND in the kind of soul revue, including DJs and support acts, that Motown and Stax had brought to Europe in the 1960s and, as we've seen, soon became de-facto members.

With 'Precious', the horns that had driven 'Absolute Beginners' and appeared sporadically over the last year or so became fundamental to the tune. The body of the song is over in two and a half minutes, but the twisty horn solos stretch the song to over four minutes for the album version without it going anywhere. But I guess that's what funk is, find your groove and stick to it like glue. To those fans who thought The Jam should simply rewrite 'Going Underground' ad infinitum, it was a difficult pill to swallow, and for those who saw the band as a 1960s mod tribute act with bolshy lyrics, their minds were already made up. Weller realised that a new breed of open, inquisitive fans was going to be difficult to attract and, in that sense, The Jam had to go.

'Just Who Is The Five O'Clock Hero?' (Weller)
Produced by Pete Wilson
7" Dutch import cat. no. 2059 504
12" Dutch import cat. no. 2141 558
Release date: 11 June 1982
Highest UK chart position: 8

> Hello darling, I'm home again,
> Covered in shit and aches and pains.

Once again, Weller nails the song in the opening lines. Propelled by a scattergun drumming performance from Buckler, 'Five O'Clock Hero' treads the same lyrical path as 'Town Called Malice'; people like you and me, trying to get by and seeing few results from a day's graft except perhaps an ability to pay the bills:

> It seems a constant struggle just to exist,
> Scrimping and saving and crossing off lists.

The song was released as a single in the Netherlands (only the fourth to be released there, the others being 'Going Underground', 'Town Called Malice' and 'That's Entertainment') following a successful European tour, but due to an overwhelming demand from fans in the UK, it reached number eight on the British chart, an unprecedented achievement for an import single.

Although a mention of Prince Philip might date the song, the content is, sadly, as pertinent today as it was in 1982. As I write this at the beginning of 2023, the UK is riven by strikes as (another) Conservative government presides over the country, where people are literally having to choose between paying for heat or paying for food. The more things change, the more they stay the same.

'Trans-Global Express' (Weller)
Never one for shying away from nicking a good tune when he heard it, here Weller recreates the horn riff, the melody, the sentiment and even the 'ba-ba-bas' 0f The World Column's 1969 northern soul stomper 'So Is The Sun'.

That this song meant a lot to Weller is obvious – the band's 1982 tour in March and April was the Trans-Global Express tour ('I hope this tour is the fucking shake up' he wrote in his programme notes) and the words were printed on the inside sleeve of the album on the opposite side to the rest of the lyrics, their isolation giving them more importance. Weller was using the song to make a statement that he wanted to be heard loud and clear. When you consider this, it's a shame the song's mix is so muddled; introduced by another spoken '1, 2, 3, 4', the vocal is barely audible, the backing track cacophonous but not in a good way. Its pile on of different ideas, of sounds, both musical and vocal (there are a few ska vocal motifs going on at one point) means clarity is surrendered.

The theme of 'Trans-Global Express' is of the working man and woman taking back power from the lazy, bloated political elite that:

Keep us divided with their greed and hate,
Keep you struggling to put the food on your plate.

Weller had been criticised before as some kind of 'champagne socialist'. It's a common accusation against people with left-leaning political tendencies who make more money than the 'average' person, but a limited number of people giving away their money wouldn't help society as a whole. What would help is our benevolent leaders using their powers to make everyone's life that little bit easier, not just those who donate wads of cash to political parties. Weller never said he had the answers, but he could at least highlight the issues.

In the end, Weller's open question...

Imagine if tomorrow the workers went on strike,
Who would earn their profits?
Who would make their bombs?

...was always likely to fall on deaf ears, and the plea to the police and armed forces, 'you men in uniform'...

Not to turn against your own kind,
Whenever governments tell you to.

...was never likely to come to fruition. But you can only try. The 'fucking shake-up' that Weller had asked for was a pipedream as far as wider society was concerned, but by now, he had his own ideas of what that shake-up might be, and he made it clear in the last lines of the song where he's addressing the words as much to himself as to the population,

The responsibility you must bear,
When it's your own future in your hands,
May be a hard one to face up to,
But at least you will own yourself.

'Running On The Spot' (Weller)

Although at the time *The Gift* was released, no one outside the band's coterie knew The Jam were on the verge of splitting up, 'Running On The Spot' was a telling outlet of Weller's frustrations of where the band were in relation to the army of fans that hung on his every word but never really seemed to listen:

> I was hoping we'd make real progress,
> But it seems we have lost the power,
> Any tiny step of advancement,
> Is like a raindrop falling into the ocean,
> We're running on the spot, always have, always will.

If a backing track has the ability to be ironic, then this is as good an example as you might find. Introduced yet again with Weller's '1, 2, 3, 4' (how many is that now?), four-to-the-floor snare, thumping bass and the descending guitar line that Weller employs often but always to good effect, musically it does anything but stand still. The urgency of the music stands at odds with the caustic, complaining lyrical content, but when one is placed against the other, it makes for a 'classic' Jam track. As the song comes to an end, the music fades out, leaving the vocals to swim around in echo so, by the end, the lyric is almost disappearing up its own backside, which may or may not be a metaphor. Or maybe they just wanted to sound like the Mamas and Papas.

Whilst researching for this book (meaning surfing the internet), I came across the following opinion about 'Running On The Spot', which perhaps echoes the sentiments of many fans but also shows why Weller had had enough by this point: 'probably the last song that Paul Weller wrote that sounds like The Jam should have been released instead of 'Bitterest Pill'.

Whatever the problems with 'Bitterest Pill', and they shall be addressed later in the book, the song at least showed Weller's willingness to experiment and to move away from 'that' sound, but even as late as 2005, when this quote is taken from, some fans still chose to misunderstand Weller and his motives. There's little wonder he wanted out.

'Circus' (Foxton)

Another instrumental, but 'Circus' at least has some coherency and direction, as opposed to an aimless jam out on tape. Written by Foxton, and featuring more of the funky, plunky bass that he was favouring from time to time, the song's melody is played by Weller. He models it very much on the style of 1950s guitar hero Duane 'The Twang's the Thang' Eddy, whilst simultaneously mimicking Nile Rogers. The track is layered with horns and percussion. In the breakdown, it steals from 'Precious', with its febrile high-pitched snare, timbale rolls and piercing whistle blasts, which, as has already been noted, had been stolen from Pigbag. The idea for the song's title comes from the view of Piccadilly Circus from the window of Air Studios where the track was recorded, and if it's a metaphor for the hustle and bustle of that London junction, it does a very creditable job.

'The Planner's Dream Goes Wrong' (Weller)

The Jam play calypso. If that sounds like an idea that should have been left in the studio, you might be right, but it does point to a band not resting on its laurels. That they had the belief, imagination and musical dexterity to introduce different genres and, if not always successful, at least to be always looking forwards is a worthy aim.

A parping trumpet and steel drums open the track before Weller gives his views on a topic that was a recurring theme, housing in general and town planning in particular. Today, in city centres across the UK, there are gleaming towers of steel and glass that attract the doyens of the middle classes under the banner of 'city living', but in the 1950s, that wasn't the case. Post-war Britain needed housing and cheap, pebble-dashed tower blocks sprung up quickly to fill that need:

They were gonna build communities
It was going to be pie in the sky

By the 1970s, many of these blocks were no-go areas and, as much as many of the people living in them (including my two grandmothers) would do their best to keep them trim, it was a losing battle to graffiti and 'piss stench hallways and broken-down lifts'. On *In The City*'s 'Bricks And Mortar', it was the man whose house cost 40 grand; here, it's 'the house in the country designs the 14th floor', but however you want to describe it, the idea remains the same: highly paid architects and planners in the green belt suburbs decide how the rest of us might like to live.

The steel drums were played by Russ Henderson, whose band had, in 1965, played at a small outdoor social event for the residents of Notting Hill in London. The event caught on, became popular and is still going today.

'Carnation' (Weller)

After the impossibly jaunty musical backing of 'Planner's Dream Goes Wrong', we're back on more familiar Jam territory with the dark gloom of 'Carnation'. Written in the first person, lyrically, it's devastatingly critical of the person singing the words.

I trample down all life in my wake,
I eat it up and take the cake,
I just avert my eyes to the pain,
Of someone's loss helping my gain.

Indeed, the lyrics are so profoundly cold and depressing, you might imagine it's the Devil himself who's giving you an honest description of his own character failings, of which there are many, and a stark warning of what's to come if you follow this infernal manifestation,

Touch my heart and feel winter,
Hold my hand and be doomed forever.

There follows a piano solo played out in harsh single notes, following the melody line, with none of the frills that might be expected when a piano is introduced to the mix; this is resolutely one-finger playing. As the song rumbles to its end, propelled by Buckler's skittish snare rolls, and as the listener plays with ideas as to who can be singing this nihilistic paean to greed, the truth is exposed:

And if you're wondering by now who I am,
Look no further than the mirror,
Because I am the Greed and Fear,
And every ounce of Hate in you.

That 'Greed', 'Fear' and 'Hate' are purposefully given uppercase initial letters, making them personal pronouns, hardens the imagery through the song, and tells us these are not just emotions but are figures that walk among us and must be guarded against. The song fades out with simple la-la-las, in the way a small child might stick his fingers in his ears and 'la-la-la' because they don't want to listen to what's being told to them. Are Jam fans just putting their fingers in their ears to the messages Weller has spent half a decade trying to get across? There's little wonder his patience was wearing thin.

'Town Called Malice' (Weller)
7" double A-side (with 'Precious') cat. no. POSP 400
12" double A-side (with 'Precious (extended)') cat. no. POSPX 400
Produced by Pete Wilson and The Jam
UK release date: 11 January 1982
Highest UK chart position: 1
The Jam song that people don't know they know: 'it goes 'da, da, da, da-da, da, da, da, da-da'', 'oh', comes the reply, 'that one. Yeah, I like that one'. 'Town Called Malice' became the third Jam single to enter the charts at the top, and it stayed there for three weeks, the longest run of the band's four number-ones.

With its instantly recognisable (a little bit knicked from The Supremes' 'You Can't Hurry Love') bass line and the Hammond organ fill, 'Town Called Malice' swings straight from the off. As the dancefloor fills to a, somewhat unusually for The Jam, song you can dance to, Weller enters the fray to remind you that this is, in fact, 1982, not 1968,

You'd better stop dreaming of the quiet life,
'Cos it's the one we'll never know.

What a downer. Although Weller was thinking of his hometown of Woking when he wrote the song, it's the most 'northern' song from a band who were, it seemed to me, resolutely 'London'. The images Weller creates are pure *Coronation Street*, woollen and steel mills, coal mines and back-to-back housing. (I'm sure back-to-backs existed in the South, but that was beyond my understanding at the time.) The sleeve photo was taken by (an uncredited) Rick Buckler from the tour bus and is a grimy sepia-tone image of close-knit housing with, superimposed, the frame of a factory window with all the glass panels smashed, or perhaps they're prison bars.

At one point, Weller addresses the housewife who was so near breaking point in 'Private Hell':

A hundred lonely housewives clutch empty milk bottles to their hearts.
Hanging out their old love letters on the line to dry,
It's enough to make you stop believing when tears come fast and furious.

But it's not just the housewives, it's everyone and the decisions that must be made when work is hard to find, and money is difficult to earn.

A whole street's belief in Sunday's roast beef,
Gets dashed against the Co-op.
To either cut down on beer or the kid's new gear,
It's a big decision in a town called Malice.

Whatever, the message is clearly spelled out, none of this is your fault: 'Stop apologising for the things you've never done'.

After the single had gone straight to the top of the charts, *Top Of The Pops* invited the band to play both tracks back-to-back on one episode. It was the first time a band had done this since The Beatles with 'Day Tripper'/'We Can Work It Out' in 1965. In Weller's longstanding quest to make The Jam bigger than The Beatles it was another step forward, but time was against him.

Accompanying the release came the band's most slick video to date. Filmed with a soft focus, Foxton chose a very 1960s semi-acoustic bass and Weller, with his mod-tastic French line haircut, dropped the Rickenbacker to concentrate on being Otis Redding, in spirit if not in delivery. If Weller's growing frustration with the band's fans and their 'lad's night out' behaviour at gigs, wasn't generally known outside the group's circle, the two inserts into the video are clear enough, 'Anti-complacency league, baby!' and 'If we ain't getting through to you, you obviously ain't listening!'. If it wasn't clear to the fans themselves, it was to Weller; they were certainly complacent, and they certainly weren't listening.

The video also introduced Steve Nichol (here playing the Hammond in white woollen gloves but really a trumpet player) and Keith Thomas (tapping away on a tambourine but really a saxophone player), though their respective skills would be put to greater use on the flip side of the single.

It's worth mentioning that for all the slickness of the band's video, if you really want to know what 'Town Called Malice' is about, check out its use in the 2000 film, *Billy Elliot*. The scene opens with the song's bass riff and Billy's brother, Tony (Jamie Draven), in a stand-up argument with Billy's dance teacher, Mrs. Wilkinson (Julie Walters), as Tony calls his young brother, Billy (Jamie Bell), 'a twat' and warns him off 'doin' anymore fuckin' ballet' before calling Mrs. Wilkinson a 'middle-class cow'. Mrs. Wilkinson responds: 'You know nothing about me, you sanctimonious shit' before Weller's vocal begins. The scene then cuts to Billy in the backyard, seething with pent-up rage, tap dancing away his anger in hobnail boots in the outside privy, and in the alley between back-to-back terraced housing, at one point windmilling his arm in pure Townshend fashion. It's a young boy's frustration at small-minded people and a longing for escape, he limps up a drab street with the (surely digitally altered) clear blue North Sea behind him; this snapshot does more to tell the story of the song than any pop video ever could.

Throughout this book, reference has been made to the fact that The Jam didn't particularly like America, and the feeling was for the most part, mutual. But in 2017, a film was released in the US to little fanfare called *Fun Mom Dinner* (5.3/10 on *imdb*) with the tagline 'Every mom needs a time out'. 'So what?', you reasonably ask. One of the songs on the soundtrack is 'Town Called Malice'. How the song relates to the film, I'm afraid to find out but without wishing to denigrate something I've never seen, I'm willing to go out on a limb and suggest that for every use of a song that's worthwhile, there's one that is not. I could be wrong, though.

Back in the UK, the fact that 'Town Called Malice' became the band's signature tune shows how the British public, on the face of it, care little about the content of lyrics and will always lean towards a pumping dance number.

'The Gift' (Weller)
'Move, move, we got the gift of life'.

The album comes to a rousing close with an invitation, or is it a plea, to 'keep on moving, we gotta keep moving'. Although fans were unaware at the time, The Jam, in the mind of Weller at least, had had their time and their race was run. Feeling ever more constrained by the limitations of a three-piece – notwithstanding Nichol and Thomas's contributions – and the expectations of both the public and critics alike.

The Jam's final album track is clicked in by Buckler before a swirling Hammond organ, reminiscent of original Mod favourites the Small Faces, washes over the track that is propelled by meaty, beaty, big and bouncy bass and drums. In fact, the mid-song breakdown, which Buckler and Foxton start playing alone, has a most Steve Marriott-like R&B guitar solo. As you listen to the lyrics, you can feel the desperation in Weller: 'Think of the future, and make it grow'.

For all The Jam's influences and the large amount of soul and R&B cover versions taken from black music, the band – given their background, understandably – remained a resolutely 'white' band. Their audience was made up of mostly white, working-class kids but if you really want to encompass all the Jam were trying to achieve, you had to open up a little.

Take a pinch of white and a pinch of black,
Mix it together, make your heart feel better.

Weller was still keen to promote togetherness, harmony and, most of all, peaceful solutions to intractable problems, but, ultimately, as simply a musician in a band, he'd come to realise that if even the people who listened to him the most didn't get the message, then who would? And as *The Gift* fades out with an improvised call-and-response between Weller and Foxton, and people chatting over the cacophonous music, which always brought to my mind the noise of a party, The Jam were all but finished.

'The Great Depression' (Weller)
B-side to 'Just Who Is The Five O'Clock Hero'
Recorded at AIR Studios, London
Produced by The Jam and Tony Taverner
That The Jam could 'waste' a song such as 'The Great Depression' on the B-side of an import-only single does one of two things; it either shows that the band were on such a roll of quality tunes that even something as great as this could be summarily dismissed, or someone, somewhere lost the plot. Maybe it's a bit (a lot) of both.

On first listening, it's a jaunty number with lots of opportunity for handclaps a la many a northern soul tune, and after the first chorus, a horn section to buttress its soul credentials. It shows the direction the band were moving, but too many Jam fans were still shouting for the power three-piece of 'When You're Young' and 'Going Underground' and, Weller felt, were never going to accept his attempts to re-invent the band towards a more soulful sound. It certainly exasperated Weller, who had never been a punk; that was simply a bandwagon that came along at the right time for The Jam to hitch their trailer to. He had grown up with soul, as indeed had the original mods, with all the mod bands of the 1960s plundering labels such as Motown and Stax for singles and album tracks. (As has already been mentioned, Weller said in an interview during a tour to promote *Setting Sons*, 'We didn't climb aboard the wagon, all of a sudden, we were being quoted as a new wave band.' Given the musical mood of the times, and The

Jam's explosive playing, they were obviously going to be bundled up in the movement and complaining about it after the event seems moot.)

If the music of 'The Great Depression' captured the free spirit of the '60s, a cursory glance at the lyrics shows Weller in anything but a celebratory soul boy mood:

I think we must have all gone mad,
Maybe right turned over.
They promise us the earth,
Instead we've got the great depression.

It's 1982, the Conservatives under Margaret Thatcher are in power, Yuppies rule London and everyone wants everything right now. But why?

No sense of purpose in the competition,
Keeping up with the Joneses.
You buy a house, you buy a car,
You buy a marriage and a bed of roses.

Consumerism has swamped the UK and Weller, on a beach somewhere in Italy, has decided it's time to end the struggle.

An interesting side note to the recording is that Tony Taverner is credited with a co-production with the band. There is no mention of Taverner on any other Jam recording, but a quick internet search tells us he's been 'active' since the late 1960s and that most of his credits have been as an engineer, as opposed to a producer, having worked with, among a host of others, Wham! and Duran Duran. Whatever his input into this particular track, the result is extremely good. It's light and punchy and could have, should have, been an A-side.

'War' (Whitfield/Strong)

B-side to 'Just Who Is The 5 O'Clock Hero?'

The details behind this first version of Edwin Starr's 'War' have been impossible to come by. The band released the song as part of the bonus single that accompanied 'Beat Surrender', but this version is totally different. Available only on the 12" version of '5 O'Clock Hero', it's altogether more forceful and dynamic than the later version. Opening with the chant, 'War, huh, what is it good for? (Absolutely) nothing', sung by the band (as opposed to the female duo Afrodiziac, who begin the newer version, and who imbue it with more natural grace and 'soul'), it's gruff and accusatory and precedes a stomping musical backing; wah-wah funk guitars, throbbing bass, hi-hat sixteenths and a single crashing snare to each bar.

Throughout this book, I've generally been quite critical of The Jam's treatment of covers, but their natural tendency to bludgeon their way through absolutely works in their favour here, the song's lyrical content invites an aggressive delivery that works well in juxtaposition to the pacifist call in the lyrics themselves.

The song is set for an extended run, a la 'Precious', but comes to an abrupt 'huh' end and the echo and reverb repeat so often that the word almost turns into a police siren. Make of that what you will.

'The Bitterest Pill (I Ever Had To Swallow)' (Weller)

7" cat. no. POSP 505
Recorded at Maison Rouge Studios, London
Produced by Pete Wilson and The Jam
UK release date: 10 September 1982
Highest UK chart position: 2
Guest musician:
Jenny McKeown: vocals

Known in the media as something of a miserable old git, and not without reason, the humour (or sarcasm, which to me are pretty much the same thing) in Weller's writing often goes unseen. Taken at face value, 'Bitterest Pill' is a love song, actually a lost-love song, and the excruciatingly embarrassing video supports the idea, but the lyrics are run through with biting sarcasm and, somewhat unsurprisingly, bitterness. They are also so ridiculously overly poetic it's difficult to see how they could be read without humour. Perhaps Weller's back catalogue of literal writing, painting graphic pictures and telling kitchen sink dramas rooted in real life meant critics couldn't see the playful side,

> When the wheel of fortune broke, you fell to me,
> Out of grey skies to change my misery,
> The vacant spot, your beating heart took its place,
> But now I watch smoke leave my lips and fill an empty room.

Written when Weller was seriously thinking of leaving the band and, by definition, breaking the band up, The Jam were contracted to write at least two more singles. If that sounds more like a job than being in a band, once you sign 'the deal' it amounts to the same thing. Although 'Malice' had been an incredible success among both the fans and media, 'Precious' was disconcerting for some of the band's vast number of followers and 'Bitterest Pill' did nothing to allay that concern. Opening with a familiar Weller descending chord motif sounding eerily like the theme of the BBC children's TV series *Bagpuss* (Bagpuss was a fat, furry stop-motion cat in case you missed the show), the first lines tell you exactly who this song is aimed at,

> In your white lace and your wedding bells,
> You look the picture of contented new wealth.

Told in the first person, the anger and bitterness felt by the betrayal of an old girlfriend could well have hit a mark if anyone had really cared. Sweeping strings and a falsetto vocal attempt to add some '70s soul into the proceedings, and Jennie McKeown, of The Belle Stars, gamely adds passion into her vocal to try and alleviate the song from a crushing maudlin dirge – the humour in the lyrics notwithstanding – but she's fighting a losing battle. Musically, nothing was sounding quite right; it was The Jam, but it wasn't. Even the reviewer in teen music magazine *Smash Hits* was unimpressed. 'Come on Weller, you can do better than this!'

The video was also a break from the band's no-nonsense 'performance-in-front-of-the-camera' style and required them to approximate acting, a terrible decision on someone's part. The scene where Weller, in a ball of anger and frustration, smashes his fist down on a park's café table, is so wooden you could burn it on a log fire. With its Miss Havisham-esque beginning, dark streets and open fires, it's uncomfortable to watch in its cheesiness.

Although the single reached number two on the charts, it was simply a result of the number of fans who would buy anything The Jam released (me included, I had no quality control as far as The Jam were concerned) and, although we might have wished for better, we were happy with anything, though I admit here that I like the song. The cover star, gazing longingly in black and white at a lone window, is Vaughn Toulouse, singer with Department S whose 1981 single 'Is Vic There?' reached number 22 in the UK chart. Toulouse became friendly with Weller and DJ'd at some Jam shows. He later signed to Weller's Respond record label, and in 1983, released 'Fickle Public Speakin'' as The Main T Possee, with lyrics by himself, and Weller credited with the music and production. Toulouse died in 1991 from an AIDS-related illness at just 32 years old.

'Pity Poor Alfie' (Weller), 'Fever' (Davenport, Cooley)
B-side to 'The Bitterest Pill (I Ever Had To Swallow)'
The swing's the thing. Although the band were heading towards the break-up, it was clear they could still come up with a mighty tune, and here we have another B-side that could have been an A-side. Most Weller lyrics are straightforward, written with a style and maturity way beyond his years, but the subject matter of 'Pity Poor Alfie' is far from clear, and the words seem to be a series of non-sequiturs that somehow became a song.

Cause we were sleeping in the noonday sun,
We escaped the test and the marathon run,
And no one heard and these mournful cries of 'Alfie!'
We put a stop to that.

But it's a very good song. The upbeat bounce of the backing track, with brash trumpets that, played using a mute, turn slightly sleazy as the track goes on, could easily have been the theme tune to a 1960s film (maybe that's why the title character is called Alfie?) and in that fact, they have something in common with more than one or two other Jam tracks.

'Alfie' segues effortlessly into 'Fever'. Originally released by Little Willie John in 1956, it's Peggy Lee's 1958 version that most people recognise as it became synonymous with the singer and was a Top-Five hit in the UK at the time. Although the song has been covered by numerous artists from Elvis to Madonna to Beyoncé, it's a jazz number at heart and the plinky-plonk piano and the same muted cornet used on 'Alfie', playing a snake-like improvised solo, give The Jam's version an authentic jazz feel and the song is played with a reverence seldom found in a Jam cover.

Beginning in the summer of 1982, rumours had begun to swirl around the music press that all was not well in The Jam camp. It was being reported that the band were headed for a split and, in the way of the press, when solid facts are absent, fevered speculation will do. To quell the increasing noise, Weller finally made a statement:

This is a personal address to all our fans. At the end of this year, The Jam will officially be splitting up, as I feel we have achieved all we can together as a group. I mean this both musically and commercially.

I want all we have achieved to count for something and most of all I'd hate us to end up old and embarrassing like so many other groups do. The longer a group continues the more frightening the thought of ever ending it becomes – that is why so many of them carry on until they become meaningless. I've never wanted The Jam to get to this stage.

What we (and you) have built up has meant something, for me it stands for honesty, passion and energy and youth. I want it to stay that way and maybe exist as a guideline for new young groups coming up to improve and expand on. This would make it even more worthwhile.

I have written this as a direct contact with you and so you hear it from us first. But also to say thank you for all the faith you have shown in us and the building of such a strong force and feeling that all three of us have felt and been touched by.

Here's to the future. In love and friendship.
Paul Weller (Oct. 1982)

And so, the speculation came to an end, here it was in black and white. To thousands of fans like me who never looked much past each record as it was released and didn't see the bigger picture, and despite the earlier rumours, it was a seismic shock. The Jam were the biggest band in the country, they'd just had their first number-one album at the sixth time of asking. And, crucially, they still had something to say at a time when much of the charts was filled with songs about Goody Two Shoes and a woman called Rio who danced on the sand. I mean, really, who gave a shit about that. But as was always apparent to those who knew him more closely than the fans, whether personally or professionally, Weller was a stubborn man and once his mind was made up, it was made up. That was that.

If anyone reading this book wasn't around at the time and might question just what a story the breakup was, it made the BBC evening news. Yet this was no teen band calling it a day, leaving a trail of exaggerated hysteria behind them, nor was it the type of laughably hyped Oasis/Blur non-story concocted by the music industry and media to shift a few more units. This was a band who spoke for those of us without a voice, who sang about a Britain that we recognised as the place we lived and about a society we were part of. This was a band whose like we would never see again because the times that made them would never be repeated. Let's cut back to the news story.

The Jam have announced they're breaking up. The group are led by singer and songwriter Paul Weller. At 24, he's become something of a spokesman for the new beat generation. He's pronounced on politics, life and music to fans so enthusiastic to receive his message that they've come from America and Japan to hear him. We went to meet Mr. Weller just before he finally unjammed The Jam.

The journalist asked a simple question, 'Why stop now?'

I feel we've achieved enough. We've done all we can do as the three of us and I think it's a good time to finish it. I don't want to drag it on and go on for like, y'know, the next 20 years and become nothing and mean nothing and end up like the rest of the groups. I want us to count for something. I want everything I've done for the last five or six years to count for something.

On the face of it, it was an astonishingly brave decision, but it was the only decision possible to give The Jam the legacy they deserved.

'Beat Surrender' (Weller)
7" cat. no. POSP 540, 7" double pack cat. no. POSPJ 540, 12" cat. no. POSPX 540
Recorded at Maison Rouge Studios, London
Produced by Pete Wilson
UK release date: 26 November 1982
Highest UK Chart Position: 1
Guest musician:
Tracie Young: vocals
When The Jam released their last ever single, the cat had officially been out of the bag for a month or so and the still disbelieving fans took 'Beat Surrender' straight to number one, their third 7" to achieve that distinction (although 'Start!' reached the top of the chart, it entered at number three).

It's a valedictory, brass and piano blowout with the guitar so low down in the mix it might as well not be there and despite so many Jam songs being led and anchored by Foxton and Buckler, it was Weller's power chords and slashing rhythms that gave the songs so much colour. Shorn of the Rickenbacker (or whatever guitar Weller was recording with at the time) the song falls flat. Another anomaly is the vocals. The Weller/Foxton vocal blend had worked so well, so many times before but here was something different. 'Beat Surrender' is a call-and-response tune, in the R&B style the band had borrowed from so often in the past, perfect for The Jam, but you can clearly hear that Weller is singing his own backing vocal. Perhaps Foxton was unavailable for the recording, or perhaps the split had rattled Foxton and Buckler so much that being in the studio was a painful experience. Whatever the truth, to me at the time, it proved there was something unsavoury within the band set-up.

For all the misgivings Weller had about The Jam, 'Beat Surrender' is still a call to arms for fans, take those dreams of yours and do something about them,

All the things that I shout about (but never act upon),
All the courage and the dreams that I have (but seem to wait so long).

However, the optimism and joy that the single purports to espouse are lacking in the *Top Of The Pops* performance, where Weller, looking lost without his guitar, as he always did, appears only to remember he's supposed to be promoting the song as the second verse kicks in. He's so uninvolved that he mimes the original lyric 'bullshit', having evidently forgotten that the BBC had ridiculously insisted it be substituted by 'bullfrogs' for the transmission, which at least adds a little comedy to the whole affair. (Indeed, it's the most unenthusiastic television appearance from a musician since Weller's own non-performance on the same programme's New Year's Day 1981 special when he hangovered his way through 'Going Underground'.) Guest vocalist Tracie Young, soon to release her own songs on Weller's Respond label, and only there because, in Weller's words, the exposure would be good for her, is game, but as all eyes are inevitably on the singer, it's a battle that is lost before it's begun. And to add insult to what is already an almost terminal injury, Foxton has chosen to play an Aria bass. Foxton was never the coolest (*that* haircut), but the Rickenbacker 4001 and the Fender Precision were cool. An Aria? The final knife in the chest came when he played the same instrument on The Jam's last live TV appearance on *The Tube*. Oh Bruce, how could you?

The single was released in a gatefold format to accommodate a bonus 7" and Weller's sleeve notes, under the guise of The Boy Wonder, are upbeat and positive:

Understand, kiddiwinks, that there are times, undoubtedly, when it's a kick to be alive, when life isn't all doubt and futility, misery and hurt but an adrenalin provider such as you find in the cold air of winter which you can gasp into your lungs, feeling the air pump your body full of strength, bringing a smile of confidence supreme to your lips as it pays homage to your youth instincts.

And so, Weller comes full circle, talking of youth, the power of the collective, standing up for yourself and for each other against 'The Man' and keeping the flame alive.

And if you feel there's no passion,
No quality sensation,
Seize the young determination,
Show the fakers you ain't foolin,
You'll see me come runnin,
To the sound of your strummin,
Fill my heart with joy and gladness,
I've lived too long in shadows of sadness.

'Shopping' (Weller)
7" B-side to 'Beat Surrender'

If fans were wondering exactly where Weller would go post-Jam, the answer really begins here. Buckler opens the track, but whereas in the past you would have expected explosive drumming, it's jazz brushes that shuffle in, quickly followed by jazz/blues trumpets and a tricksy walking bassline from Foxton; it's got The Style Council written all over it.

As in 'Beat Surrender', it's clear that Weller is doing his own backing vocals in this cynical take on consumerism,

Something about my face,
Must just be the wrong shape,
I'd better buy another brand pretty quick.

The vocal delivery is almost whispered, another seismic change from a typical Jam song, and from the upbeat insistency of the A-side. If anyone was still in denial that Weller intended to leave the Jam 'sound' far behind, the track ends with an extended flute solo. I'll write that again for clarity, an extended flute solo. Ron Burgundy would be proud.

12" B-side and bonus 7" single; 'Move On Up' (Mayfield), 'Stoned Out Of My Mind' (Record, Acklin), 'War' (Whitfield, Strong)
Afrodiziac guest vocals on 'War'

The A-side of the bonus single opens with The Jam's take on Cutis Mayfield's 'Move On Up'. Unsurprisingly, Weller avoids the temptation to follow Mayfield's gentle falsetto and opts for a more forceful rendition, following the high-pitched horn riff that opens the song. Following on from the influence of Pigbag on the 'Precious' bassline, there is a dropdown in the song, resplendent with frantic percussion and whistles, that is, and not for the first time, a straight steal from 'Papa's Got A Brand New Pigbag'. If someone has an idea that you like, why not go the whole hog and nick the lot? The percussive frenzy notwithstanding, though Mayfield's original has congas breathlessly pushing the song forward, it's a fairly faithful copy, but the lyrical content echoes that of 'Beat Surrender', the title of the song enough to enlighten the listener as to what Weller is hoping his fan base might do.

'Stoned Out Of My Mind', a 1973 Top Ten hit for the Chi-Lites, has Weller attempting a croon. It's almost there, but not quite. It's among Weller's most restrained vocal performances on a Jam recording and is a comfortable match for the overall sound, more brushes from Buckler, horn stabs and a mellow bass. There's nothing remarkable in the song; no politics or polemic, no urging us to be better or more open; to be less constrained by societal norms, and it's all the better for it.

The second recorded version of 'War' is a very different affair to that on the B-side of the '5 O'Clock Hero' 12". Here, Weller's vocal is so quiet it's almost lost in the mix, but the music itself has a laid-back '70s funk/soul feel, with an awful lot of plucked bass from Foxton. Generally, when performing cover versions, The Jam rarely tried to imitate the feel of the originals, preferring a more 'smash and grab' approach, but this follows the music of the rest of this bonus EP in its deference to what had come before. In a similar fashion to the first version of 'War', the song seems set for a lengthy instrumental workout, but suddenly, wreathed in echo and reverb, the track ends in anticlimactic fashion.

If you listen to the band's songs in chronological order and listen to the B-sides after the A-sides, this is the last note that The Jam play on record during their career. It's an unsatisfactory end in that respect and so my advice would be to listen to 'Beat Surrender' and let the pulsating fade-out, four-to-the-floor drums and 'up and at 'em' brass lead you into the future.

On 22 January 1983, Polydor re-released all of The Jam's 16 singles, including the imports '5 O'Clock Hero' and 'That's Entertainment'. 12 of them made the charts, staying around for an aggregate of 53 weeks.

Thought That I Would Forget You? Postscript

It's now over 40 years since The Jam called it a day and yet, as we've seen over the course of this book, their music continues to pop up in unexpected places; soundtracking TV shows, dramas and films. When a producer or director requires music that will resonate with a certain demographic (terrible word) or remind us of the frankly horrible state of Britain in the late 1970s and early 1980s, The Jam won't be far from their commercial minds. This leaves us questioning how The Jam came to have such a long-lasting legacy.

I think the reasons have been covered in the preceding pages, but let's recap; youth and the positivity of youth they promoted over almost everything else made them different. That they had something to say to their fans (us) was different and although we didn't always heed the words, or even understand them, it didn't stop Weller from trying to reach us right up to the very end. The times that the band operated in made them, as Nina Simone said when asked about the subject matter of her songs during the late 1960s as the drive for racial equality in the US grew, 'How can you be an artist and not reflect the times?'

The Jam had integrity by the bucketload, it finally being one of the reasons for the split. How do you keep writing and singing about youth and the need for individualism when you're approaching your mid-20s and are in the nation's biggest band, swallowed up in the write-record-tour cycle of mainstream acts? When you've become all you used to find so disagreeable about the music industry. And the split itself; despite the fact they were making genuine ground in the US and Europe, Weller saw the band had gone as far as it could and the decent thing to do was to stop. It sounds simple, and it is I suppose, but put yourself in the same situation and what would you have done?

Did The Jam become as big as The Beatles? Had Weller's dream of only a few years earlier come to fruition? (And we must remember that all of what has been written in this book happened over the course of only five years). Of course not. Who could ever be bigger than The Beatles? But they broke, or at least equalled, Beatle records for songs in the charts concurrently and for *Top Of The Pops* appearances. And much like The Beatles, they influenced their contemporaries and continue to influence bands and musicians now, decades after their breakup. So no, not bigger than. But perhaps, in the UK at least, equal to?

This leaves us with the thorny question: what were The Jam? I've been asked this question many times, most recently by foreign students I teach English to and to whom The Jam is a new name. Were they rock? Well, I suppose they were in a generic sense but no, not really. Punk then? Sort of, to begin with, but no, not really. New wave? Mod? Pop? I refer you to my previous answers.

Frustrated by my inability to label the band, they ask what songs they should listen to – and how do you answer that? 'In The City'? 'Tube Station'?

'Going Underground'? 'Absolute Beginners'? 'Precious'? How do you define a band that changed so much in so short a space of time by recommending a song or two? In the end, I decided there's only one true answer to the question, what were The Jam? Well, they were The Jam.

It's Mixed With Happiness, It's Mixed With Tears – A Selection Of Post-Career Jam Releases

Dig The New Breed
LP cat. no. POLD 5075
Produced by Peter Wilson
UK release date: 10 December 1982
Highest UK chart position: 2

Side 1: 'In The City' (recorded at the 100 Club; 11 September 1977), 'All Mod Cons', 'To Be Someone', 'It's Too Bad' (The Rainbow, London; 13 December 1979), 'Start' (sic), 'Big Bird', 'Set The House Ablaze' (Hammersmith Palais, London; 14 December 1981)
Side 2: 'Ghosts' (Bingley Hall, Birmingham; 21 March 1982), 'Standards' (Reading University; 16 February 1979), 'In The Crowd' (Edinburgh Playhouse; 6 April 1982), 'Going Underground', 'Dreams Of Children', 'That's Entertainment', 'Private Hell' (Glasgow Apollo; 8 April 1982)

When Weller decided to split the band, they were still contracted to Polydor for two albums. *The Gift* saw them halfway, but Weller's enthusiasm had disappeared, and as another studio album was out of the question, fans were given the contractual obligation album, otherwise known as *Dig The New Breed*. Released on 11 December 1982, the day before The Jam's last ever show in Brighton, *Dig The New Breed* adds to the list of live Jam tracks on official releases. The songs are in chronological order except for the strange positioning of 'Standards', recorded at Reading University in 1979, which follows a March 1982 version of 'Ghosts', and is before an April 1982 recording of 'In The Crowd' from the Edinburgh Playhouse. I find this a weird placement, or maybe I'm missing something. What it does do is neatly showcase how much the band had improved as musicians in a relatively short time, and that the material on *Modern World* doesn't stand up to the later works, but I think that is old news. The only song that hadn't already been released as a single or album track is Eddie Floyd's 1968 soul stomper 'Big Bird'. Recorded at the Hammersmith Palais on 14 December 1981, and with a brass section added for authenticity, it's more restrained than the band's earlier blood and guts covers and is all the better for it. Of course, the problem with the entire album is that an actual gig is a snapshot in time and the feel of a live show – the volume, the sweat, the excitement – can't be reproduced on vinyl, no matter how good a band were live. And The Jam were among the best. A single line from a *Smash Hits* review (7½ out of 10) written by Neil Tennant (who would soon become a global superstar as frontman of the Pet Shop Boys) sums it up succinctly: 'You can't ask for more from a live LP'.

The album sleeve has (uncredited) illustrations of Weller, Foxton and Buckler and returns to the *All Mod Cons*/Immediate records font. The middle cut-out is a throwback to when singles were mainly sold in simple paper sleeves with a hole so you could read the label and see who the artist and song title. There is also a humorous nod to the 1960s with the information the album has been 'Electrically Recorded Live; play it on all phonographs'.

On the rear of the album are sleeve notes from the band. Buckler makes a comment about the nature of a live album:

Playing live, to me, is still the root of all music; it can be and should be a spontaneous and exciting event for those involved, but to capture this atmosphere on record is near impossible for obvious reasons.

Foxton goes for the personal angle:

Loyalty from the fans has always surprised and amazed me. This album is especially for you.

Weller is more stylised, settling for a greatest hits of memories through the years in a 'That's Entertainment' list kind of way before ending, 'What have I learnt? 'BELIEF IS ALL!''

The inside sleeve has a selection of photos covering the band's career. There were no lyrics this time, but we all knew them anyway by now.

(A final postscript on *Dig The New Breed*; on the tracklisting – the album sleeve, the inner sleeve and the record label – 'Start!' is missing its exclamation mark. Call me pedantic, and you wouldn't be the first, but I find this annoying.)

Snap!
Double LP cat. no. SNAP1
UK Release Date: 14 October 1983
Highest UK Chart Position: 2

Side 1: 'In The City', 'Away From The Numbers', 'All Around The World', 'The Modern World', 'News Of The World', 'Billy Hunt', 'English Rose', 'Mr. Clean'
Side 2: 'David Watts', ''A' Bomb In Wardour Street', 'Down In The Tube Station At Midnight', 'Strange Town', 'The Butterfly Collector', 'When You're Young', 'Smithers-Jones' (7" version), 'Thick As Thieves'
Side 3: 'The Eton Rifles' (7" version), 'Going Underground', 'Dreams Of Children', 'That's Entertainment', 'Start!' (7" version), 'Man In The Corner Shop', 'Funeral Pyre'
Side 4: 'Absolute Beginners', 'Tales From The Riverbank', 'Town Called Malice', 'Precious' (7" version), 'The Bitterest Pill (I Ever Had To Swallow)', 'Beat Surrender'

Despite being released almost a full year after the band had called it a day, The Jam proved their musical legacy was no flash-in-the-pan and the still vast number of fans, many of whom had decamped to The Style Council, took the album to number two.

The vinyl version of the album came in a gatefold sleeve with extracts from the band's authorised biography, *A Beat Concerto,* written by long-time friend and fan Paolo Hewitt. Each side of the inner sleeve has notes from 'Lucky Horses' (I can't tell you who Lucky Horses is/are, but I assume it's not Weller because he would be talking about himself in the third person, and that's no way to behave) which are a little over-stylised for my taste and strangely dismissive when talking about the *Modern World* period:

Listless, no vision, splashing around in the pond of mediocrity, nearly drowning...

If nothing else, you have to give them kudos for their honesty, though Lucky Horses does hit the nail on the head towards the end when asking what the band could do next:

Pull off the unexpected? Surprise and subvert? How can they? The stage set is too big, the context too constricted and the playing too familiar. Even saxophones, keyboards and new voices can't infiltrate the nucleus. Stifled and sullen...

As a release, it adds little. All the singles are here and some good choice of album tracks. For anyone new to the band at the time, this was an excellent introduction, though many other *Greatest Hits* have since been available and, of course, we have Spotify. For those who bought *Snap!* when it was released, initial quantities saw the inclusion of a 7" four-track live EP taken from shows at Wembley Arena from the band's *Beat Surrender* tour (the farewell tour) on the 2 and 3 December. The track listing is 'Move On Up', 'Get Yourself Together', 'The Great Depression' and 'But I'm Different Now'.

As three of the four tracks had already been on different releases, I've spoken about them already, but the addition of a little-known Small Faces number, 'Get Yourself Together', is an interesting choice and, as it turns up on the *Extras* album, I'll talk a little about it then.

The design of the album sleeve and the colours used give *Snap!* a distinct 1960s vibe, but the most notable thing is the band photo on the front cover in which Weller is smiling. Smiling!

Extras
LP cat. no. 513177-1
UK Release Date: 6 April 1992
Highest UK Chart Position: 15

'The Dreams Of Children', 'Tales From The Riverbank', 'Liza Radley' (demo version), 'Move On Up', 'Shopping', 'Smithers-Jones' (single version), 'Pop

129

Art Poem', 'Boy About Town' (alternate version), 'A Solid Bond In Your Heart' (alternate demo version), 'No One In The World', 'And Your Bird Can Sing', 'Burning Sky' (demo version), 'Thick As Thieves' (demo version), 'Disguises' (remixed version), 'Get Yourself Together' (remixed demo version), 'The Butterfly Collector', 'The Great Depression', 'Stoned Out Of My Mind', 'Pity Poor Alfie/Fever', 'But I'm Different Now', 'I Got You (I Feel Good)' (demo version), 'Hey Mister', 'Saturday's Kids' (demo version), 'We've Only Started' (remixed version), 'So Sad About Us', 'The Eton Rifles' (demo version)

It's difficult to know where to start talking about an album such as *Extras*. It's such an unbalanced affair featuring different mixes of unknown tracks, original versions of tracks that any Jam fan would already own but are 'extra' in so much as they were only B-sides or album tracks, and demos that have some value for the fan but don't stand up to repeated listens.

The demo versions are, to me, proof positive that for all of Weller's claims that sometimes his demos were better than the final band version, this is demonstrably untrue. There's a world of difference between a 'raw', unpolished sound and a bloke knocking out an idea on a guitar. The Jam were three individuals who all brought their own 'thing' to the party and created a sum larger than its parts, and we'd do well to remember that.

'Pop Art Poem' (Weller)
This is a genuine curiosity. Given away as a flexidisc in yellow, green or blue (mine's yellow) with the short-lived magazine *Flexipop,* the tune (it's not really a song at all) is a casual jazz pastiche with Weller giving a lazy spoken vocal over the top. At the end, he says, 'I made this up as I went along. It's good, innit'. No Paul, it isn't. It's bloody awful.

'A Solid Bond In Your Heart' (Weller)
Pencilled as the last Jam single, it ended up as the fourth Style Council single and the two versions are considerably different. This version opens with a glockenspiel and, with its brass stabs in the drop-down, is so desperate to be a genuine Northern soul single, and so accurate is it in its reimagining that it could actually be one. It has 'authentic' written all over it. The recording is almost releasable quality, but the bass line is lumpy and detracts from the flow.

'No One In The World' (Weller)
This track turned up a few years later as a 'hidden' number on the Jam tribute album *Fire & Skill*. Weller sings in his best Surrey accent and at the top of his register. There's a five-chord sequence towards the end of the song that is a blatant steal from The Beatles' 'Michelle'. I invite the reader to draw their own conclusions.

'And Your Bird Can Sing' (Lennon, McCartney)
Taken from The Beatles' (best album) *Revolver*, I've always believed attempting to cover any Beatles song is a hiding to nothing. How do you better Beatles versions of Beatles songs? Simply, you can't. This is a too-straight copy, though all the subtlety of the original is lost. Of course, this isn't a finished version, and we must take that into account, but this is not a song you'd ever want to try to cover. That Weller, in his 'ten guitarists' list written around 1981, had 'the guitar work on *Revolver*' as his number nine might explain why he was keen to make the attempt.

'Get Yourself Together' (Marriott, Lane)
'Get Yourself Together' is a little-known Small Faces song and, given Weller's longstanding love affair with mod, and that his publishing imprint had brought out a small book on the Small Faces in 1982 (which he did a poor job of plugging whilst being interviewed before the band's last live TV appearance on *The Tube*), and given that Steve Marriott was number seven on his 'ten guitarists' list, it's strange that The Jam never released a Small Faces cover. 'Get Yourself Together' receives a typical Jam treatment, which is they attempt to flatten it but, here, that treatment works. The drums are urgent and insistent, and the vocal delivery is enthusiastic. It's very much a two-minute mod pop song and The Jam don't overdo it. The track was released in a live form on the bonus 7" that came with the *Snap!* album.

'I Got You' (I Feel Good) (Brown)
Reminds us that Paul Weller isn't James Brown.

'Hey Mister' (Weller)
Delivered as voice and piano, it's a dig at politicians, 'you're just so smug in your elected seat'. There are some good individual lines, 'you juggle lives around with the stroke of a pen', but the song ends abruptly as Weller ran out of words, and he clearly never went back to it again. Which is a shame as it has the bones of something worth listening to.

'We've Only Just Started' (Weller)
The last song on *Extras* that is worth giving your time to is 'We've Only Just Started'. Beginning with a simultaneous guitar and bass run and the drums giving accents, it's at once very familiar and not quite right. Then the drums kick in fully on a four-to-the-floor beat, and it dawns on the listener that this is 'Tales From The Riverbank' on speed. The melody is the same, the lyrics are different and the backing track pounds along until a clumsy middle-eight destroys the momentum before the song picks it up again for the end. Someone had the good sense to recognise the basis of an excellent song, but this version isn't it. Whoever decided to swap the speed for acid did the song, and the listener, a huge service.

131

Direction, Reaction, Creation
Five CD box set cat. no. 537 143 2
UK Release Date: 26 May 1997
Highest UK Chart Position: 8

CD five: 'In The City', 'Time For Truth', 'Sounds From The Street', 'So Sad About Us', 'Worlds Apart', 'Billy Hunt', 'It's Too Bad', 'David Watts', 'Best Of Both Worlds', 'That's Entertainment', 'Rain', 'Dream Time', 'Dead End Street', 'Stand By Me', 'Every Little Bit Hurts', 'Tales From The Riverbank', 'Walking In Heaven's Sunshine', 'Precious', 'Pity Poor Alfie', 'The Bitterest Pill (I Ever Had To Swallow)', 'A Solid Bond In Your Heart'

Direction, Reaction, Creation is a handsome package. Five CDs, each in their own gatefold sleeve, and each sleeve picturing one of Weller's Rickenbackers through the ages. There's a comprehensive booklet covering the tracks, gigs and releases of the band, and for someone who wants an instant Jam collection, look no further. CDs one to four are the band's official releases in chronological order and have already been covered in the book therefore I don't see a reason to list them all again, it would be tedious to write and to read. The fifth disc has some remixed versions of tracks and alternate takes, but it does have some interesting Weller material and some interesting covers and it's those that I'm going to look at.

'Worlds Apart' (Weller)
Recorded in February of 1978, 'Worlds Apart' is a simple rolling piano riff that, to me at least, evokes The Monkees. There's nothing special to grab the listener's attention until the song reaches the bridge when it suddenly becomes 'Strange Town' before returning to the original riff. As an insight into the musical development of a song, it's certainly intriguing, but not a lot else.

'Best Of Both Worlds' (Foxton)
Recorded in September 1979, the spiky guitar lick is very new wave, and very of its time. In early 1979, during a break from touring, Foxton had come across a band playing in a pub near where he lived and offered them a joint management deal with himself and John Weller at the helm. The band were The Vapors and, following a support tour with The Jam, they found themselves in the Top Five with their single 'Turning Japanese'. I mention this because 'Best Of Both Worlds' sounds more like The Vapors than The Jam. In case you were wondering, this is not a good thing.

'Rain' (Lennon, McCartney)
Weller made another incursion into Lennon and McCartney territory with 'Rain'. Recorded in April 1980 with soon-to-be Jam producer Pete Wilson on drums and Hammond organ, it's a ponderous version of a song that, in its original

form, swings like the swingin' sixties itself. It also shows us that, generally speaking, Weller's voice is at its best when he's singing his own songs.

'Dead End Street' (Davies)
Also recorded in 1980, here Weller copies another of his songwriting idols, Ray Davies, with The Kinks' 'Dead End Street'. Pete Wilson opens the track with a hard, staccato piano line, very similar to the original and the song follows along the same lines. It's a decent effort, but you're left asking yourself, what's the point? Weller later said of this period that, during downtime, he and Wilson used to go to the studio and mess around making demos, and why wouldn't you?

'Stand By Me' (Lieber, Stoller)
Covering soul tunes that are so standard, so well known, is a questionable activity and there are few soul tunes quite so standard as Ben E. King's 'Stand By Me'. The recording date is unknown, but as Pete Wilson is again involved, we can assume it's from the same period as 'Rain' and 'Dead End Street'. There is a wall of reverb on the swirling organ, but then the drums enter in the very definition of 'ploddy', and a harsh, chopping guitar enters the fray and you have to stop the song and go for a lie-down. It's pretty bad.

'Every Little Bit Hurts' (Cobb)
Although originally recorded by Brenda Holloway in 1964, it was the Spencer Davis Group who took 'Every Little Bit Hurts' to number 41 on the charts the following year. This piano-led gospel number is given every bit of respect it deserves by Weller. Recorded in August 1981, it shows what people rarely heard through Jam songs and that is Weller can actually sing a bit. This tune pushes his register as far as it will go and is all the better for it. Having previously written how Weller sings his best when singing his own songs, this is the exception to prove the rule.

'Walking In Heaven's Sunshine' (Weller)
There is no recording date available for this harmless outtake from a 1960s film soundtrack. Think Mini Coopers, mini-skirts, and long shots of the Houses of Parliament over the opening titles. It's light, breezy and, laden as it is with woo-hoos and ba ba bas, makes me think of ace mods, The Action.

When the box set was released in the US in 2006, reviewer Joe Tangari felt the need to quickly introduce the band to America:

> It can be tough for Americans to understand just how huge The Jam were in Britain, given their near-total lack of success in the States, but here's an indication: After the group disbanded, all 16 of their UK singles we reissued by Polydor and all 16 of them re-charted *at the same time*.

133

I sometimes think it's not just Americans that need to be reminded of this fact.

Fire & Skill – The Songs Of The Jam
LP cat. no. IGNCD 3
Executive Producer: Simon Halfon
UK Release Date: 1 November 1999
Highest UK Chart Position: 12
Stitched together for the end of the Millennium/Christmas market, *Fire & Skill* saw a variety of bands giving their own interpretation of The Jam's back catalogue, and all choices were written by Weller. It's a hit-and-miss affair, with some artists giving the songs a completely new twist and some playing it straight with a turn of the melody here and there in an attempt at individuality. Weller gives the album his tacit approval by supplying the last song, albeit as a 'hidden' track and I can't help thinking he'd not heard the album when he agreed to appear on it. Despite the overall questionable quality, that it made number 12 on the charts is yet another example of the unceasing popularity of the band.

'Carnation' – Liam Gallagher and Steve Craddock
Double A-side CD single with 'Going Underground' cat. no. IGNSCD16
UK Release Date: 23 October 1999
Highest UK Chart Position: 6
This is what AI and ChatGPT would come up with if they'd been programmed to write a 'psychedelic' song. Opening with the Oasis frontman's solo vocal, it descends into a lifeless drudge of a tune. Ocean Colour Scene and Weller guitarist Craddock is firmly in the back seat, though the slide guitar in the drop-down offers a glimpse of his contribution. Big piano chords give it an appearance of life, but the backwards vocal is so kitsch it makes your teeth hurt. That it got to number six in the charts is everything to do with Gallagher's status at the time and nothing at all to do with the treatment of the song.

A question that might be worth pondering; how do you have a double A-side CD?

'Start!' – The Beastie Boys featuring Miho Hatori
For a band who specialise in shouting, The Beastie Boys come straight out of left field with this, an almost instrumental take on 'Start!' The melody line, played on what sounds like a melodeon, together with Hammond organ stabs, lends it a very 1960s feel. The bass line is intact, it had to be, and the slip snare gives it a 'Madchester' edge. Japanese singer Miho Hatori's 'If I never ever see you' is ethereal and longing, giving a nice counterpoint to the swing of the number. If the idea of a cover is to re-imagine a song, the Beasties nail it.

'That's Entertainment' – Reef

Glastonbury's second most famous export – they broke the charts and my will to live with 'Place Your Hands' – get something of a short straw. The Jam's version is a straight four-chord affair that musically doesn't go anywhere, but rather than attempt to bring some imagination to the track, Reef take a leaf from The Jam's 'how to tackle a cover version' handbook and crush the life out if it. There's even a '1-2-3-4' intro to give it a live feel, and for all I know, it could have been recorded live, but it's basically rubbish.

'The Gift' – Heavy Stereo

Talking of rubbish... Heavy Stereo's main man, Gem Archer, would find a level of recognition when he joined Oasis, but first, he served up this terrible take on what was always a fairly average track. When you look at The Jam's back catalogue, some of the songs on this album are strange choices (as are the artists), but nevertheless, the original material offers something to work with. Heavy Stereo pass up the opportunity to create something new, and the choppy guitar in the song's breakdown is plain awful.

'Art School' – Silver Sun

Silver Sun follow The Jam's intro to the opening track on their debut album with a '1-2-3-4' (presumably, they didn't know Reef were going to do the same thing). However, where Weller imbues it with the energy that was the trademark of *In The City*, Silver Sun's is the weakest ever put to record. Once the track begins, though, Silver Sun layer sweet harmonies across a song that in the Jam's version, is a gruff punch of a tune.

'English Rose' – Everything But The Girl

A song that was written for Tracey Thorn to sing. Her bandmate Ben Watt plays it straight and for once, that's a good choice. Weller was obviously a fan as Thorn appeared on The Style Council's debut LP *Café Bleu* with her version of 'Paris Match', which she mercifully sings entirely in English.

'Going Underground' – Buffalo Tom

Double A-side CD single with 'Carnation' cat. no. IGNSCD16
UK Release Date: 23 October 1999
Highest UK Chart Position: 6

Giving an unapologetic guitar track by a three-piece band to another three-piece band seems like a recipe for dullness, but Boston, Massachusetts' Buffalo Tom put a very different spin on 'Going Underground'. On a very average album, this track stands out as a glorious example of what can be done with a cover version, something The Jam themselves could have learnt a lesson or two from. Rather than a straight copy, Buffalo Tom have taken a blistering, attack of a song and gently turned it into a uniformly paced lament, there are no 'hey, la, la, la, la's here. Singer Bill Janovitz gives the vocal a yearning in direct contrast to the original and, against bassist Chris Colbourn's softer backing vocals, gruffly wonders what went wrong and yearns to leave it all behind.

The song was released as a double-A side with Liam Gallagher and Steve Craddock's rendition of 'Carnation'. It says a lot about Buffalo Tom's track that whoever chose to include it on the release ignored other more obvious names more well-known to a UK audience. To this day, this version of 'Going Underground' is one of my favourite covers, not just of The Jam, but of any song.

'The Butterfly Collector' – Garbage

The Scottish/American hybrid band sold over 17 million albums in their decade-long career, which ended in 2005 (they reformed in 2010 to record a fifth album). Fronted by Edinburgh-born Shirley Manson, Garbage take 'The Butterfly Collector' and turn it into electronica, Manson deadpanning her way through the melody, which is almost a straight copy of the original, though where Weller sings 'You've got no pride', Garbage change it to 'You've got no brains'. Why?

When I was a student in the late 1990s, I was one of many 'journalists' from student papers invited to interview Garbage when they appeared at Doncaster Dome. In an attempt at being cleverly humorous, I had planned on asking Manson why she was only happy when it rained. Fortunately for me, Manson didn't grace the interview, so instead, I turned to the band's drummer Butch Vig who had been the producer on Nirvana's *Nevermind* album and, apologising for the question not being about Garbage, asked if he and Nirvana realised what an impact *Nevermind* and 'Smells Like Teen Spirit' would have on music. He smiled and said, 'Yes'.

'The Modern World' – Ben Harper

One of the stranger artist choices. Harper's polite delivery sounds at odds with the track that we all have in our heads, and not in a good way, as the melody never alters a note. Weller's rough and ready guitar solo is replaced by a far too well played 'rock' solo, and the chance to give the song some of the edge that it's crying out for is thrown away with, 'I don't give a damn about your review'. A wasted opportunity.

'Town Called Malice' – Gene

If 'That's Entertainment' was a short straw for Reef, Britpop chancers Gene get the shortest straw of all. What can you do with what has become arguably The Jam's signature tune? You can attempt a different arrangement, and starting the track with Hammond organ rather than the overly familiar bass line gives the impression that Gene are going to give us something a little more individualistic. But no, it's The Jam's version, but with wobbly vocals from Martin Rossiter that stretch some lyrics to breaking point. Poor.

'To Be Someone' – Noel Gallagher

Bringing the album to a close (or so we assume) is Liam's brother and sometime Weller collaborator, Noel Gallagher. As the brains behind Oasis, Gallagher Senior knew how to put a big tune together, but here goes for the acoustic treatment. The melody changes here and there to show willingness, but it's generally a straight rendition except for the last chorus. Where Weller sings, 'So I stay confined to my lonely room', Gallagher chooses the more opulent, 'Sitting on my own in my expensive yacht'. Despite the strained vocal, it lacks the bite of the original and clearly shows that Liam is by far the better singer in the family.

'No One In The World' – Paul Weller

A cheeky, unmentioned addition is this slice of whimsy that first appeared in demo form on the *Extras* album. There's an air of nostalgia that works better for the distance between The Jam and this release and it brings the album to a contented end.

How Are Things In Your Little World? The Jam In Numbers

To round up the band's career in number form, here are a few figures that give an insight to what they created in those five short years.

UK singles released – 16
Number one singles – 4
Weeks singles spent on the UK Top 40 – 116
UK albums released – 6
Number one albums – 1
Weeks albums spent in the UK Top 40 – 107
Songs with swear words (fuck, fucking, bastard, shit, cock, etc.) – 18
Songs with a scratch along the bottom E string – 19
Songs that switch between pick-ups, like Pete Townshend – 10
Songs that don't have the song title in the lyric – 7

Read All About It – Bibliography And Places Of Interest

Hewitt, P., *The Jam: A Beat Concerto – the Authorised Biography* (Riot Stories 1983)
Willmott, G., *Sounds From The Street* (Reynolds & Hearn Ltd. 2003)
Honeyford, P., *The Modern World By Numbers* (Eel Pie Publishing Ltd. 1980)

Documentaries
About The Young Idea (Dir. Bob Smeaton; Channel X 2015)
The Making Of All Mod Cons (Dir. Don Letts; Diamond Film Ltd. 2006)
The Jam: Punk Icons (Dir. Bob Carruthers; Coda 2014)

On Track series

Allman Brothers Band – Andrew Wild 978-1-78952-252-5
Tori Amos – Lisa Torem 978-1-78952-142-9
Aphex Twin – Beau Waddell 978-1-78952-267-9
Asia – Peter Braidis 978-1-78952-099-6
Badfinger – Robert Day-Webb 978-1-878952-176-4
Barclay James Harvest – Keith and Monica Domone 978-1-78952-067-5
Beck – Arthur Lizie 978-1-78952-258-7
The Beatles – Andrew Wild 978-1-78952-009-5
The Beatles Solo 1969-1980 – Andrew Wild 978-1-78952-030-9
Blue Oyster Cult – Jacob Holm-Lupo 978-1-78952-007-1
Blur – Matt Bishop 978-178952-164-1
Marc Bolan and T.Rex – Peter Gallagher 978-1-78952-124-5
Kate Bush – Bill Thomas 978-1-78952-097-2
Camel – Hamish Kuzminski 978-1-78952-040-8
Captain Beefheart – Opher Goodwin 978-1-78952-235-8
Caravan – Andy Boot 978-1-78952-127-6
Cardiacs – Eric Benac 978-1-78952-131-3
Nick Cave and The Bad Seeds – Dominic Sanderson 978-1-78952-240-2
Eric Clapton Solo – Andrew Wild 978-1-78952-141-2
The Clash – Nick Assirati 978-1-78952-077-4
Elvis Costello and The Attractions – Georg Purvis 978-1-78952-129-0
Crosby, Stills and Nash – Andrew Wild 978-1-78952-039-2
Creedence Clearwater Revival – Tony Thompson 978-178952-237-2
The Damned – Morgan Brown 978-1-78952-136-8
Deep Purple and Rainbow 1968-79 – Steve Pilkington 978-1-78952-002-6
Dire Straits – Andrew Wild 978-1-78952-044-6
The Doors – Tony Thompson 978-1-78952-137-5
Dream Theater – Jordan Blum 978-1-78952-050-7
Eagles – John Van der Kiste 978-1-78952-260-0
Earth, Wind and Fire – Bud Wilkins 978-1-78952-272-3
Electric Light Orchestra – Barry Delve 978-1-78952-152-8
Emerson Lake and Palmer – Mike Goode 978-1-78952-000-2
Fairport Convention – Kevan Furbank 978-1-78952-051-4
Peter Gabriel – Graeme Scarfe 978-1-78952-138-2
Genesis – Stuart MacFarlane 978-1-78952-005-7
Gentle Giant – Gary Steel 978-1-78952-058-3
Gong – Kevan Furbank 978-1-78952-082-8
Green Day – William E. Spevack 978-1-78952-261-7
Hall and Oates – Ian Abrahams 978-1-78952-167-2
Hawkwind – Duncan Harris 978-1-78952-052-1
Peter Hammill – Richard Rees Jones 978-1-78952-163-4
Roy Harper – Opher Goodwin 978-1-78952-130-6

Jimi Hendrix – Emma Stott 978-1-78952-175-7
The Hollies – Andrew Darlington 978-1-78952-159-7
Horslips – Richard James 978-1-78952-263-1
The Human League and The Sheffield Scene –
Andrew Darlington 978-1-78952-186-3
The Incredible String Band – Tim Moon 978-1-78952-107-8
Iron Maiden – Steve Pilkington 978-1-78952-061-3
Joe Jackson – Richard James 978-1-78952-189-4
Jefferson Airplane – Richard Butterworth 978-1-78952-143-6
Jethro Tull – Jordan Blum 978-1-78952-016-3
Elton John in the 1970s – Peter Kearns 978-1-78952-034-7
Billy Joel – Lisa Torem 978-1-78952-183-2
Judas Priest – John Tucker 978-1-78952-018-7
Kansas – Kevin Cummings 978-1-78952-057-6
The Kinks – Martin Hutchinson 978-1-78952-172-6
Korn – Matt Karpe 978-1-78952-153-5
Led Zeppelin – Steve Pilkington 978-1-78952-151-1
Level 42 – Matt Philips 978-1-78952-102-3
Little Feat – Georg Purvis - 978-1-78952-168-9
Aimee Mann – Jez Rowden 978-1-78952-036-1
Joni Mitchell – Peter Kearns 978-1-78952-081-1
The Moody Blues – Geoffrey Feakes 978-1-78952-042-2
Motorhead – Duncan Harris 978-1-78952-173-3
Nektar – Scott Meze – 978-1-78952-257-0
New Order – Dennis Remmer – 978-1-78952-249-5
Nightwish – Simon McMurdo – 978-1-78952-270-9
Laura Nyro – Philip Ward 978-1-78952-182-5
Mike Oldfield – Ryan Yard 978-1-78952-060-6
Opeth – Jordan Blum 978-1-78-952-166-5
Pearl Jam – Ben L. Connor 978-1-78952-188-7
Tom Petty – Richard James 978-1-78952-128-3
Pink Floyd – Richard Butterworth 978-1-78952-242-6
The Police – Pete Braidis 978-1-78952-158-0
Porcupine Tree – Nick Holmes 978-1-78952-144-3
Queen – Andrew Wild 978-1-78952-003-3
Radiohead – William Allen 978-1-78952-149-8
Rancid – Paul Matts 989-1-78952-187-0
Renaissance – David Detmer 978-1-78952-062-0
REO Speedwagon – Jim Romag 978-1-78952-262-4
The Rolling Stones 1963-80 – Steve Pilkington 978-1-78952-017-0
The Smiths and Morrissey – Tommy Gunnarsson 978-1-78952-140-5
Spirit – Rev. Keith A. Gordon – 978-1-78952- 248-8
Stackridge – Alan Draper 978-1-78952-232-7

Status Quo the Frantic Four Years – Richard James 978-1-78952-160-3
Steely Dan – Jez Rowden 978-1-78952-043-9
Steve Hackett – Geoffrey Feakes 978-1-78952-098-9
Tears For Fears – Paul Clark - 978-178952-238-9
Thin Lizzy – Graeme Stroud 978-1-78952-064-4
Tool – Matt Karpe 978-1-78952-234-1
Toto – Jacob Holm-Lupo 978-1-78952-019-4
U2 – Eoghan Lyng 978-1-78952-078-1
UFO – Richard James 978-1-78952-073-6
Van Der Graaf Generator – Dan Coffey 978-1-78952-031-6
Van Halen – Morgan Brown – 9781-78952-256-3
The Who – Geoffrey Feakes 978-1-78952-076-7
Roy Wood and the Move – James R Turner 978-1-78952-008-8
Yes – Stephen Lambe 978-1-78952-001-9
Frank Zappa 1966 to 1979 – Eric Benac 978-1-78952-033-0
Warren Zevon – Peter Gallagher 978-1-78952-170-2
10CC – Peter Kearns 978-1-78952-054-5

Decades Series

The Bee Gees in the 1960s – Andrew Mon Hughes et al 978-1-78952-148-1
The Bee Gees in the 1970s – Andrew Mon Hughes et al 978-1-78952-179-5
Black Sabbath in the 1970s – Chris Sutton 978-1-78952-171-9
Britpop – Peter Richard Adams and Matt Pooler 978-1-78952-169-6
Phil Collins in the 1980s – Andrew Wild 978-1-78952-185-6
Alice Cooper in the 1970s – Chris Sutton 978-1-78952-104-7
Alice Cooper in the 1980s – Chris Sutton 978-1-78952-259-4
Curved Air in the 1970s – Laura Shenton 978-1-78952-069-9
Donovan in the 1960s – Jeff Fitzgerald 978-1-78952-233-4
Bob Dylan in the 1980s – Don Klees 978-1-78952-157-3
Brian Eno in the 1970s – Gary Parsons 978-1-78952-239-6
Faith No More in the 1990s – Matt Karpe 978-1-78952-250-1
Fleetwood Mac in the 1970s – Andrew Wild 978-1-78952-105-4
Fleetwood Mac in the 1980s – Don Klees 978-178952-254-9
Focus in the 1970s – Stephen Lambe 978-1-78952-079-8
Free and Bad Company in the 1970s – John Van der Kiste 978-1-78952-178-8
Genesis in the 1970s – Bill Thomas 978178952-146-7
George Harrison in the 1970s – Eoghan Lyng 978-1-78952-174-0
Kiss in the 1970s – Peter Gallagher 978-1-78952-246-4
Manfred Mann's Earth Band in the 1970s – John Van der Kiste 978178952-243-3
Marillion in the 1980s – Nathaniel Webb 978-1-78952-065-1
Van Morrison in the 1970s – Peter Childs - 978-1-78952-241-9
Mott the Hoople and Ian Hunter in the 1970s –
John Van der Kiste 978-1-78-952-162-7

Pink Floyd In The 1970s – Georg Purvis 978-1-78952-072-9
Suzi Quatro in the 1970s – Darren Johnson 978-1-78952-236-5
Queen in the 1970s – James Griffiths 978-1-78952-265-5
Roxy Music in the 1970s – Dave Thompson 978-1-78952-180-1
Slade in the 1970s – Darren Johnson 978-1-78952-268-6
Status Quo in the 1980s – Greg Harper 978-1-78952-244-0
Tangerine Dream in the 1970s – Stephen Palmer 978-1-78952-161-0
The Sweet in the 1970s – Darren Johnson 978-1-78952-139-9
Uriah Heep in the 1970s – Steve Pilkington 978-1-78952-103-0
Van der Graaf Generator in the 1970s – Steve Pilkington 978-1-78952-245-7
Rick Wakeman in the 1970s – Geoffrey Feakes 978-1-78952-264-8
Yes in the 1980s – Stephen Lambe with David Watkinson 978-1-78952-125-2

On Screen series
Carry On... – Stephen Lambe 978-1-78952-004-0
David Cronenberg – Patrick Chapman 978-1-78952-071-2
Doctor Who: The David Tennant Years – Jamie Hailstone 978-1-78952-066-8
James Bond – Andrew Wild 978-1-78952-010-1
Monty Python – Steve Pilkington 978-1-78952-047-7
Seinfeld Seasons 1 to 5 – Stephen Lambe 978-1-78952-012-5

Other Books
1967: A Year In Psychedelic Rock 978-1-78952-155-9
1970: A Year In Rock – John Van der Kiste 978-1-78952-147-4
1973: The Golden Year of Progressive Rock 978-1-78952-165-8
Babysitting A Band On The Rocks – G.D. Praetorius 978-1-78952-106-1
Eric Clapton Sessions – Andrew Wild 978-1-78952-177-1
Derek Taylor: For Your Radioactive Children –
Andrew Darlington 978-1-78952-038-5
The Golden Road: The Recording History of The Grateful Dead – John Kilbride 978-1-78952-156-6
Iggy and The Stooges On Stage 1967-1974 – Per Nilsen 978-1-78952-101-6
Jon Anderson and the Warriors – the road to Yes –
David Watkinson 978-1-78952-059-0
Magic: The David Paton Story – David Paton 978-1-78952-266-2
Misty: The Music of Johnny Mathis – Jakob Baekgaard 978-1-78952-247-1
Nu Metal: A Definitive Guide – Matt Karpe 978-1-78952-063-7
Tommy Bolin: In and Out of Deep Purple – Laura Shenton 978-1-78952-070-5
Maximum Darkness – Deke Leonard 978-1-78952-048-4
The Twang Dynasty – Deke Leonard 978-1-78952-049-1

and many more to come!